Light of Light

Light of Light

How Trinitarian Theology Became a Thing, and Why It Matters

Johannes Aakjær Steenbuch

CASCADE *Books* • Eugene, Oregon

LIGHT OF LIGHT
How Trinitarian Theology Became a Thing, and Why It Matters

Cascade Books
An Imprint of Wipf and Stock Publishers
199 W. 8th Ave., Suite 3
Eugene, OR 97401

www.wipfandstock.com

PAPERBACK ISBN: 979-8-3852-5503-0
HARDCOVER ISBN: 979-8-3852-5504-7
EBOOK ISBN: 979-8-3852-5505-4

Cataloguing-in-Publication data:

Names: Steenbuch, Johannes Aakjær, author.

Title: Light of light : how trinitarian theology became a thing, and why it matters / Johannes Aakjær Steenbuch.

Description: Eugene, OR : Cascade Books, 2026 | Includes bibliographical references.

Identifiers: ISBN 979-8-3852-5503-0 (paperback) | ISBN 979-8-3852-5504-7 (hardcover) | ISBN 979-8-3852-5505-4 (ebook)

Subjects: LCSH: Trinity. | Theology, Doctrinal.

Classification: BT111.3 .S875 2026 (paperback) | BT111.3 (ebook)

VERSION NUMBER 03/09/26

We believe in one God, the Father Almighty,
creator of all things visible and invisible.

And in one Lord, Jesus Christ, the Son of God, begotten of the Father, only-begotten, that is, of the being of the Father, God of God, light of light, true God of true God, begotten, not made, the same being as the Father, by whom all things were made, both in heaven and on earth, who for us humans and for our salvation descended and became flesh and was made human, suffered and rose on the third day and ascended into heaven, from where he comes to judge the living and the dead.

And in the Holy Spirit.

—*The Nicene Creed*, Nicaea year 325

Contents

Preface

THIS BOOK WAS WRITTEN on the occasion of the 1700th anniversary of the council of Nicea and the Nicene Creed in 325. It is not an impartial historical account, but depicts the development of trinitarian theology with an eye to what is now seen as the classical doctrine of the Trinity. It does so, however, without completely smoothing out the theological diversity, conflicts and breakthroughs that formed the background for later orthodoxy. Although the book is intended as an introduction to trinitarian theology in early Christianity, it also touches on a number of other themes, such as the understanding of salvation and human nature. The chapters are organized historically, but also thematically according to the articles of the creed. The book can as such be read as an introduction to "classic" dogmatics.

The text is written from what I like to think of as a predominantly Lutheran-ecumenical perspective. Nevertheless, the aim is to provide a reasonably balanced presentation of Nicene theology and the development of the doctrine of the Trinity up to and including the fourth century. To be sure, the book specifically tells the history of *theology*, not, for example, the church or its order in its larger political context—although it could be argued that such matters should have been taken into account. However, while today religion is often seen as the product of sociological and political circumstances, many of the available sources from the period do engage specifically with doctrine, and reading them on their own terms must mean to engage with the ideas themselves. This I have done in an attempt to make trinitarian theology relevant for our understanding of the Christian gospel. I have not engaged much directly in contemporary debates, though, but only sought to present the matters so that their relevance is hopefully clear to the reader.

The onset is to a large extent T. F. Torrance's reading of Nicene theology in his *The Trinitarian Faith* (1988). I have also made use of R. P. C. Hanson's *The Search for the Christian Doctrine of God* (1988), which is a major work in the genre, while having also consulted Wolfram Kinzig's *A History of Early Christian Creeds* (2024) for the latest research in the field. I have also benefited from recent works by, for example, Lewis Ayres, John Behr, Johannes Zacchuber, and Giulio Maspero. However, most of the following is readings of primary texts by the ancient theologians who helped shape what became the doctrine of the Trinity. In most cases I have made my own translations, although typically based on the available English translations. Greek and Latin phrases are only used when it can occasionally emphasize a point, while academic discussions are as far as possible omitted or packed away in the footnotes.

The book was originally published in Danish with the title *Lys af lys—trinitarisk teologi i tidlig kristendom.* I have used AI for translation purposes only, not for writing. I am indebted to Lars Sandbeck and Søren Holst, among others, for encouraging me to engage more thoroughly with the material presented below. Also thanks for comments to Laura Cæcilie Jessen, Kristoffer Garne, Anders-Christian Jacobsen (ch. 2), Nils Arne Pedersen (ch. 3), Martin Ravn, Eva Elisabeth Houth Vrangbæk (ch. 8), Thomas Reinholdt Rasmussen, Thomas Forum Lollike, Emil Hilton Saggau, Maria Munkholt Christensen, and many others. Thanks also to the Danish Institute in Athens for a working stay that made it possible to finish the book.

—Johannes Aakjær Steenbuch,
Nylars, Denmark 2025

Introduction

THE NICENE CREED IS the most widely accepted formulation of the Christian faith—at least in its final version attributed to the Council of Constantinople in 381. The Nicene Creed was originally adopted in AD 325, when Emperor Constantine convened a council in Nicaea to reach agreement on the order of the church and the central articles of the Christian faith. In the period between the two councils, the wording and meaning of the creed was hotly debated. Gradually, what became known as the classic Christian doctrine of the Trinity emerged.

Although the creed bears the mark of the time in which it was written, its wording still forms the basis for theological discussions and attempts to reformulate Christianity today. This is because the Nicene Creed touches on the very heart of Christianity—the question of who Jesus really is. In short, according to the creed, Jesus is the Son of God who became human for our salvation. But what does that mean more precisely?

In early Christian theology, the Son of God was seen as a kind of cosmic intermediary. God himself is distant and incomprehensible, but somewhere between God and the world is the Word of God, also called the Son of God. There were differing opinions as to whether the Son of God was created or eternal like God the Father. The general view was that the Son of God was subordinate to God the Father to some extent. This changed in the fourth century due to disputes about the relationship between God the Father and the Son. In Nicene theology, it became clear that the God we encounter in the Bible does not stay distant, but takes action by becoming human. That the Son of God is "light of light," "true God of true God," "of the being of the Father"—and most controversially, that the Son has the "same being" as the Father—are among the most remarkable formulations in the Nicene Creed that all express the belief that God has become human in Christ.

This may sound quite technical, but as the Scottish theologian T. F. Torrance explained in his book on Nicene theology, the creed is precisely a confession of the Christian *faith,* not just a collection of doctrines.[1] Not because everything depends on certain formulas, but the matter to which they point are of crucial importance. Nor was it, as suggested, because everything was decided at once. There continued to be theological discussions about the relationship between the Father and the Son, and only gradually was it thoroughly thought through what it actually means that God is triune.

When studying the theology of the early church, it is easy to become overwhelmed by how much the ancient theologians actually wrote. The many details in the discussion can be confusing, especially in the fourth century, when political concerns came to play a role in how theological concepts were formulated. The many nuances of the discussion indicate that it was not simply a matter of being for or against one particular view. The doctrine of the Trinity did not come out of the blue, but was the result of many years of theological and philosophical controversies. However, as will become clear in the following chapters, the Nicene Creed was not an attempt to capture the essence of God with philosophical concepts. It was fundamentally an attempt to express the gospel about the God who had become human.

In many traditional accounts of the story, the doctrine of the Trinity was implicitly present in the earliest Christian theology. The "heresies," on the other hand, were seen as deviating from the church's true teachings, which were ultimately confirmed at Nicaea. However, the story is not that simple, since the concept of God developed in Nicene theology in the fourth century was, in many ways, radically new. The doctrine of the Trinity was not in

1. Torrance, *Trinitarian Faith,* 18–46.

place from the beginning. On the other hand, this does not mean that it was a "distortion" of an original Christianity that was not trinitarian, as the story is sometimes told by critics of the doctrine of the Trinity. The point is simply that it took time to arrive at a theology that corresponded to the gospel of the God who became human in Jesus for our sake.

These questions are not only of historical interest, but also of relevance for contemporary issues of theology and faith. The following is an account of how the doctrine of the Trinity came into being, but also of why it is relevant for understanding what Christianity is fundamentally about. It is emphasized along the way how Nicene theology gradually developed an egalitarian view of divine relations—against forms of subordinationism that were increasingly perceived as heretical. As we shall see, this perspective also has consequences for how we view human relations, salvation, and so on. While contemporary debates will not be addressed directly, there will be hints here and there.

The first two chapters depict the development of trinitarian theology before the fourth century. Chapters 3 and 4 introduce the core themes of Nicene and Cappadocian theology. Chapters 5 through 7 discuss more specific theological questions related to trinitarian theology. Finally, chapter 8 briefly outlines the subsequent development of trinitarian theology. The afterword touches on a few areas of relevance for trinitarian theology today.

1

Polemical Fathers

The First Christian Apologists

IN THE TRADITIONAL DIVISION of church history, we typically distinguish between the so-called Apostolic Fathers and the Apologetic Fathers. The Apostolic Fathers took up the legacy of the early Christians and the apostles, while the Apologetic Fathers set out to defend Christianity—gradually becoming more systematic and theoretical in their approach. When reading the Apologetic Fathers, however, it becomes clear that attack was often the best defense. In fact, many of Christianity's theological concepts were formulated in polemics against alternative views. This also applies to the ideas that laid the foundation for the doctrine of the Trinity.

There are a number of statements in the Bible that could be used when theologians spoke of God as triune—for example, the Gospel of John's opening about the Word of God who was God and became human (John 1:1–18). Jesus's command to baptize in the name of the Father, Son, and Holy Spirit (Matt 28:19) also suggested a trinitarian interpretation. Several statements in the Old Testament could, with an appropriate dose of creativity, be read in a trinitarian way—for example when a psalm mentions a king who is anointed by God, but is also referred to as God (Ps 45), or when the book of Proverbs speaks of Wisdom, or Sophia, who was there before the creation of the world (Prov 8:22). A number of passages in Paul could also be read in trinitarian terms, as when Paul concludes a letter to the church in Corinth with the greeting that later became known as the Apostolic Blessing: "May the grace of the Lord Jesus Christ, and the love of God, and the fellowship of the Holy Spirit be with you all!" (2 Cor 13:13). Similar formulations can be found in the Apostolic Fathers, but it is not until the Apologetic Fathers that an actual trinitarian *theology* emerges in the more proper sense of a reflected discourse on God.

At the heart of the discussion is what we call *Christology*, the doctrine of Christ. What does it mean that Jesus is Christ, i.e., the Messiah, or the "anointed one," that the Jews were expecting? There were many answers to this question, and early Christians often drew on philosophical sources to clarify their concepts. It was typically thought that God created the world using his Word, the *logos*, that connects God and creation, and has now become human in Jesus Christ. If there is "more between heaven and earth," as we say, it must be the Word of God. However, the extent to which God's Word was itself God was debatable. The doctrine of the Trinity that later became "orthodox," was far from being in place in the early centuries of the church.

Philosophical Lenses

There has been a tendency to view the influence of Greek philosophy on early Christianity as mostly negative. According to this narrative, we begin with a "pure" Christianity that is gradually corrupted by philosophical thought. However, the situation is more complex than that. There is much evidence to suggest that the influence went both ways and that early Christians were in constant dialogue with Jewish and Greek philosophy from the beginning. In the Acts of the Apostles, Paul already made an appeal to philosophy when he gave his famous speech on the Areopagus in Athens.[1] By no means all Christians were hostile to philosophical thinking. On the contrary, many considered Christianity to be the true philosophy that completed the insights given to the Greek philosophers—if they didn't think the philosophers had stolen their ideas from Moses and the Old Testament. It should come as no surprise, then, that early Christians could draw on ideas from Greek philosophy.[2]

The Jewish philosopher Philo of Alexandria (c. 25 BC–AD 50) was a major source of inspiration for the first Christian theologians. Philo, who lived around the same time as Jesus, was known for his allegorical interpretation of Jewish Scripture, which he read philosophically. In the Septuagint, the Greek translation of the Old Testament also used by the theologians of the early church, God describes himself to Moses as "he who is" (Exod 3:14). Philo explained that as "the one who is," God is "being itself."[3] If God is the most fundamental thing there is, we cannot get around God, so to speak. For this reason, God's "ineffability" was a central theme for Philo, who could nevertheless speak of God as revealed in his Word. This tension became crucial. God "hides Himself," as the prophet Isaiah says (Isa 45:15), but reveals himself in his Word—and by God's Word, Philo meant the divine *logos*, which in Greek could also mean reason and rationality. Pre-Socratic philosophers such as Heraclitus had already described the *logos* as a principle that holds opposites in the world together. Philo borrowed the concept from Stoic philosophy and identified God's *logos* with Plato's "world soul."[4]

This made it possible to read the Bible through philosophical lenses. When Moses had to meet God in the "darkness" on Mount

1. For example, Paul quotes the Cretan philosopher Epimenides, who said of Zeus that "in him we live, we breathe and have our being" (Acts 17:27–28).

2. See Karamanolis, *Philosophy of Early Christianity*.

3. God is in Greek *to on*. Philo, *On the Change of Names* 2.7.

4. Philo, *Concerning Noah's Work as a Planter* 2.8–9. The world soul, in Latin called *anima mundi*, is the principle that, so to speak, gives life to the world. The idea has its roots in pre-Socratic philosophy. Later Platonism developed the notion of the demiurge, the creator god, who mediates the eternal ideas to the created world. See Dillon, *Middle Platonists*, 366.

Sinai (Exod 20:21), it was because God, in his ineffable being, is inaccessible to humans. But God reveals himself through his Word, the divine *logos* that created and ordered the world and now reveals God. In this way, Philo conceptualized in philosophical terms the biblical idea that we only really know God as revealed. The Word of God is an image of God, but also a "secondary god" who was involved in the creation of the world and now functions as a kind of cosmic high priest.[5] The Word of God is at once part of God and distinct from God.

This way of thinking came to characterize Christian theology in the first centuries. In so-called *logos theology*, we can distinguish between the inherent Word of God and the spoken Word of God.[6] The Word of God, the *logos,* is eternally in God, but in creation it becomes a spoken Word outside God. It is the Word that reveals God to humans and, in the Gospel of John, becomes human in Christ. The task for the Apologetic Fathers of the first centuries was to explain how this all fit together.

The Word of God—Christ, the Anointed

The Christian philosopher Justin Martyr (c. 100–165), like Philo, believed that God cannot be captured by human concepts. This is unfolded in Justin's second apology. Even words like *father* and *creator*, even the word *God*, are only indications derived from the works of God.[7] They do not say anything about what God *is*, but only something about what God *does*. The word *God* was understood by Justin as an innate sense of something inexplicable, as he puts it in his second apology. The Son of God is another term for the Word of God, which God has "begotten" (or "generated") before the creation of the world. The Son of God was with God

5. Philo can sometimes also refer to the Word of God as "first-begotten Son," "wisdom" and as the "mother" of creation. Philo, *On Husbandry* 51; Philo, *On Drunkenness* 31; Philo, *On Dreams* 1.37.214–18.

6. The *logos endiathetos* and the *logos prophorikos,* respectively. The distinction, also found in Philo, has its roots in Stoicism.

7. Justin, *Second Apology* 6.1–5.

when God, with his help, created everything, Justin explains. The Son of God is called Christ because he is "the anointed one," and because God has ordered everything through him.

Justin makes use of Christian terminology, but the basic philosophical structure is fairly familiar. Justin adds, however, that it is the Word of God, the divine *logos,* who has become human in Jesus to heal us by sharing in our suffering—and who is therefore worshiped by Christians alongside the "unbegotten and ineffable" God.[8] This, of course, is where Justin as a Christian differs most clearly from the Jewish philosophy of Philo. We cannot conceive of God's ineffable being in the abstract, but we know God through Jesus, who is the incarnate Word of God, Christ, "the anointed one."

This is justified biblically in Justin's dialogue with Trypho the Jew.[9] In the Hebrew Bible, kings and priests—sometimes even prophets—were anointed with oil when they were consecrated for their special tasks. This is the line of thought that Justin draws on when, in his discussion with Trypho, he explains what it means that Jesus is "the anointed." This required some allegorical maneuvers. For example, when Jacob in Genesis anointed the stone he had been lying on (Gen 28:18), this prefigures Christ.

Perhaps most interesting, however, is Justin's reading of Psalm 45—a wedding hymn about a king who is anointed *by* God, but who is apparently also referred to *as* God:

> Your throne, O God, will last for ever and ever;
> a scepter of justice will be the scepter of your kingdom.
> You love righteousness and hate wickedness;
> therefore God, your God, has set you above your companions
> by anointing you with the oil of joy. (Ps 45:6–7)

It's not very clear how this is to be understood. The passage is controversial because it can sound as if a human king is being addressed as God. According to Christian writers beginning from the Epistle to the Hebrews (Heb 1:8–9), this was exactly the

8. Justin, *Second Apology* 13.

9. Justin, *Dialogue with Trypho* 86.1–3.

case.[10] Jesus Christ is the King who is anointed by God, but is also himself God in some sense. As the Son of God, Christ is not just anointed—as so many are—but Christ is *the* anointed one, Justin explained. All other kings and anointed ones have received their share of the titles of *kings* and *anointed* from Christ. Christ, on the other hand, has received his titles directly from God the Father.[11]

This could also be tied to a notion of the Son of God as the Wisdom of God, or *Sophia* in Greek. In the book of Proverbs, Wisdom says, "The Lord brought me forth as the first of his works, before his deeds of old" (Prov 8:22). The Septuagint, the Greek translation of the Old Testament, more cryptically states, "The Lord made me the beginning of his ways for his works." This passage would become central to later discussions about trinitarian theology. Is the Son created or not? According to Justin, the passage refers to the Son of God, whom the Father had "begotten" by an act of will before creation.[12] The Son of God is, as such, divine, but also subordinate to the Father.

God, as creator and Father, is above all earthly things. For this reason, God can only be revealed through a kind of intermediary—as was the case in the bush to Moses—and this intermediary is the Son of God, who connects humans with God.[13] Like a fire that ignites new fire without changing, the Word proceeds from God, but without being cut off from God. This is the "power" that appeared to Moses in the burning thorn bush. The Son of God is called the Word because he communicates God to humans, but the Son of God is at the same time inseparable from the Father, just as the light of the sun that falls on earth is inseparable from the sun in heaven.[14] What gradually becomes a metaphor for the Son of

10. This interpretation is supported by some later Greek translations of the Old Testament, where it says that "God, O God, has anointed you," which can be read to mean that the one being addressed is also called God. See, e.g., Augustine, *Expositions on the Psalms* 45.17.

11. Justin, *Dialogue with Trypho* 86.3.

12. Justin, *Dialogue with Trypho* 61.

13. Justin, *Dialogue with Trypho* 60.

14. Justin, *Dialogue with Trypho* 128.

God as "light of light" would prove to be of central importance to later discussions.[15]

God's Hands—The Word and the Spirit

Other key figures in the development of early trinitarian theology were Theophilus of Antioch (died c. 185) and Irenaeus of Lyon (c. 125–202), both of whom engaged with philosophical discussions in their apologetical and polemical works.

In his discussions of Greek philosophy, Theophilus acknowledged that Plato in his *Timaeus* had talked about God as Father and maker of all things. Theophilus also made it clear, however, that God did not create the world out of an uncreated matter, since that would make matter eternal like God and as such impair the "monarchy" of God.[16] This line of thought laid the foundation for what became the doctrine of "creation out of nothing" (*creatio ex nihilo*).[17] God does not "need anything" to create. The world is God's good creation, Theophilus explained, poetically describing creation as a kind of anointing: "The air and everything under heaven is in a way anointed with light and spirit."[18]

God created the world using his Word, the divine *logos,* and Theophilus now speaks explicitly about the "triad" that characterizes God, in his allegorical reading of Genesis. The three days that passed before God created light, according to the story of creation, are symbols of "the three" (*trias* in Greek), says Theophilus, i.e., "God, his Word and his Wisdom."[19] Wisdom is identical with the

15. See Munkholt, "'Light from Light,'" 249–62.

16. Theophilus, *To Autolycus* 2,4. This view is found in Plato's dialogue *Timaeus*, which was widely read at the time.

17. It is disputed whether the idea is already present in Jewish thought, e.g., in 2 Macc 7:28 and Philo. The idea that creation is "in" God, who created everything out of nothing, is found in Hermas, *Pastor* 2.1.1. However, Theophilus is often credited with first clearly articulating the idea of creation out of nothing.

18. Theophilus, *To Autolycus* 1.12.

19. Theophilus, *To Autolycus* 2.15.

Holy Spirit, rather than the Son of God. Creation out of nothing is possible because God himself has what it takes to create the world. Before creation, God had his Word within him, but when God decided to create the world, he "begot" (or "generated") his Word to create the world using it.[20] God's Word is divine, but only becomes the Son of God at the creation of the world.

Irenaeus, like Theophilus, developed his thoughts in writings against a number of contemporary theological movements—especially so-called Gnosticism and Manichaeism. Irenaeus rejects the view that Jesus at some point became the Son of God when the "immutable Christ" temporarily resided in him, or that God had only apparently become human in Jesus.[21] Jesus, on the contrary, is the Son of God who became the "son of man" and suffered for us.[22] God is incomprehensible, but can be known through the love that God shows in his Word that became human in Christ to reconcile us with God.[23]

Irenaeus also has no trouble spotting Christ in the psalm about the anointed king (Ps 45). As with Justin, the psalm is about the relationship between God the Father and God the Son. However, Irenaeus adds that the anointing itself is the Spirit.[24] There is clearly something trinitarian at work. The name Christ means "the anointed one" and contains at the same time the one who anoints, the one who is anointed, and the anointing itself. This was the point, explains Irenaeus, when Jesus, quoting Isaiah, declared that "the Spirit of the Lord is upon me, because the Lord has anointed me" (Isa 61:1). The Father is the one who anoints, the Son is the one who is anointed, while the Spirit is the anointing itself.[25] The Jewish Scriptures point to Jesus Christ, whose name has a double meaning. Christ is Greek for the Hebrew Messiah, while Jesus means "savior." Both are names of deeds done, writes

20. Theophilus, *To Autolycus* 2.10.

21. So-called *adoptionism* and *docetism* respectively.

22. Irenaeus, *Against Heresies* 3.18.3.

23. Irenaeus, *Against Heresies* 4.20.4.

24. Irenaeus, *Against Heresies* 3.6.1.

25. Irenaeus, *Against Heresies* 3.18.3.

Irenaeus. Jesus is called Christ because through him the Father has "anointed and adorned all things" and because as a human being he was anointed by God in the Spirit of his Father.[26] As a human, Jesus was anointed by the Spirit of God, but the creation of the world is in a way also an anointing of everything created, as was the case in Theophilus.

In the course of his polemic, Irenaeus formulates what almost sounds like an early creed.[27] Even though the church is scattered all over the earth, it clings to the faith it has received from the apostles and their disciples, he explains. The church believes in "one God, the Father Almighty, Creator of heaven and earth and the sea and all that is in them," and in "one Christ Jesus, the Son of God, who became human for our salvation" and in "the Holy Spirit, who through the prophets proclaimed the decrees of God and things to come." These are the three key points that characterize faith according to Irenaeus. The Christian faith can be summarized by the "rule of faith," which concerns God the Father, God the Son and the Holy Spirit. This is the faith that is passed on as a tradition from the apostles through the church to the individual believer.

Irenaeus explains how God has created the world by his Word and Spirit.[28] The two are metaphorically described as God's hands: "God needed nothing to create the world, as if he had no hands of his own," says Irenaeus, "for God always has the Word and Wisdom, the Son and the Spirit, with him." It is to them that God speaks when he says in Genesis, "let us make humans in our image and likeness" (Gen 1:26). The Word and Wisdom of God are, as with Theophilus, the Son and the Holy Spirit. As the creator of the world, God is not contained by anything, but contains everything, including us and our world. When humans are created in God's "image and likeness" (Gen 1:26), it is because humans are made to resemble the Father, the Word and Wisdom—all three of which were involved in creating humanity.

26. Irenaeus, *On the Apostolic Preaching* 53.

27. Irenaeus, *Against Heresies* 1.10.1.

28. Irenaeus, *Against Heresies* 4.20.1–6.

That God did not need anything outside himself to create the world contrasts with the view that the world was created from pre-existing matter. Gnosticism and Manichaeism held views similar to Plato's, but the creator god was at best ignorant and incompetent, while matter was an evil principle—as opposed to a higher, good and immaterial God who has only now made himself known to save the elect from the world. Irenaeus's view, like that of Theophilus, is the one that became common in Christianity. The created world is not formed out of an evil, uncreated matter from which we must escape, but it is God's good creation.

The same good God who created the world out of nothing, has now let his creative Word become human to restore the broken creation. Irenaeus could speak of salvation as "recapitulation," as when Ephesians states that God's plan of salvation was "to bring unity to all things in heaven and on earth under Christ" (Eph 1:10).[29] We as humans are collectively subject to the power of death because of sin. God's Word became human to set us free from death. As Irenaeus succinctly puts it, God's Word, in his "transcendent love," has become what we are so that we can become what he is. Just as God originally formed humans with "his hands," the Word and Spirit have now joined themselves to human nature so that we can be recreated in the image and likeness of God.[30]

One Being Cohering in Three

In a Latin-speaking context, similar forms of trinitarian theology were especially developed by the North African theologian Tertullian (c. 150–220) and Roman theologians such as Hippolytus (c. 170–235) and Novatian (c. 200–250).

Tertullian is often portrayed as a sharp critic of Greek philosophy. This is not, however, because he refrained from using philosophical thought to make sense of Christianity. His reflections on the divine Trinity (*trinitas* in Latin) are influenced by Stoicism and

29. Irenaeus, *On the Apostolic Preaching* 30–31.

30. Irenaeus, *Against Heresies* 5; 5.1.3.

the tradition of Justin Martyr, Irenaeus and Theophilus. Tertullian can also speak of the belief in the Father, the Son and the Holy Spirit as the "rule of faith," that has come down to us "from the beginning of the gospel." This is how he puts it in his polemic against a theologian named Praxeas.[31] Tertullian opposes the idea that the Son and the Father are merely different sides of the same individual. Praxeas wanted to protect the one rule or the "monarchy" of God, by arguing that, since God is one, the Father and Son must be identical. This seems to have been a common belief in Rome at the turn of the third century, especially, according to Tertullian, among the "simple" believers.[32]

The view that Tertullian criticizes was also associated with contemporary theologians such as Noetus and Sabellius—hence the term *Sabellianism*, or what is more recently called *modalism*, as the Father, Son, and Holy Spirit are reduced to appearances or "modes" of the one God. The Father and the Son were not distinct persons. God the Father could perhaps even be said to become his own Son in the incarnation.[33] This posed a number of problems. If the Father and the Son are only appearances of God, it is hard to see how there can be a relationship between the two. Tertullian made it clear that the Father and the Son must be distinct individuals, although they are both God. That God rules through his Son does not diminish his sovereignty or "monarchy."[34] In Psalm 45 the king is referred to as "God." God is anointed by God, says Tertullian, so the two are clearly distinct persons, but this does not make them two gods.[35] The Father, the Son, and the Holy Spirit are all God, but distinct nevertheless.

31. Tertullian, *Against Praxeas* 2.1–2.

32. Tertullian, *Against Praxeas* 3.1. So-called *monarchianism*.

33. According to Hippolytus, Noetus believed that the Father had given birth to himself. This is probably a polemical exaggeration. Hippolytus, *Against Noetus* 1. Sabellius was condemned around the year 220 by Pope Calixtus for so-called *patripassianism*, the belief that the Father suffered on the cross.

34. Tertullian, *Against Praxeas* 3.3.

35. Tertullian, *Against Praxeas* 13.1.

Tertullian also rejects the view that the Son of God was only apparently human. That Christ has become human in Jesus is crucial to the history of salvation: If Jesus was not truly human, was God not really crucified at all? And did he not really die and rise from the dead? Tertullian states that the Son of God died, adding famously that "it must be believed because it is absurd."[36] That Jesus was buried and rose again is a certain fact, precisely because it is impossible. The point is arguably not, however, that faith is irrational or paradoxical in the modern sense, but that no one would make up a story of this kind—which is exactly what makes it credible.[37] Neither was the Trinity seen as a logical contradiction as it would be in later theology. The enemy is the philosophical rationality that excludes the involvement of God in salvation history.

Tertullian can speak of how the Son of God is called God because of his unity with the substance of God—just as the sun is present in its rays, which are in a way an extension of the sun. Christ is "God of God" just as "light of light" is lit.[38] Tertullian thus formulates the metaphor of light in a way that is later established in the Nicene Creed. He also describes God as "one substance cohering in three."[39] However, this should not be confused with a later doctrine of the Trinity, where the Father, Son, and Holy Spirit are three eternal and equal divine persons with the same being. Rather, according to Tertullian, the relationship between the Father and the Son comes about as part of the "economy" of creation and the history of salvation. God was "alone" before creation, but had within him his reason, which became Word when God spoke to create the world.[40] That Word is the Son of God, who came into being in the context of creation. There is, to this degree, a hierarchy

36. Tertullian, *On the Flesh of Christ* 5.4. Or rather, "because it is unfitting."

37. See Harrison, "I Believe Because it is Absurd."

38. Tertullian, *Apology* 21.11–12. Cf. Tertullian, *Against Praxeas* 13.10.

39. In Latin, "unam substantiam in tribus cohaerentibus." Tertullian, *Against Praxeas* 12.7. Not to be confused with the Greek *homoousios*, which in Latin would rather be *consubstantialis*. Hanson, *Search for the Christian Doctrine of God*, 102–3.

40. Tertullian, *Against Praxeas* 5.2.

among the divine persons. As water flows from a spring, the Trinity flows down from the Father, Tertullian explains, but without disturbing God's sovereignty or "monarchy."[41]

These ideas are echoed by Hippolytus and Novatian in Rome. Before creation, God had his reason and Wisdom within him, but when he decided to create the world, he gave birth to his Word as "light of light."[42] There is "one God," but while the Son is "Lord of all," the Father is Lord of him.[43] It is the Word made human in Christ that makes the invisible God visible. The Father is without beginning, while the Son comes into being with the creation of the world.[44] The Son does nothing of his own will, but obeys the commands of the Father. This avoids the problems that arise from the modalist attempt to safeguard God's monarchy by conflating the Father and the Son. Instead, we get a notion of God in which the Son is subordinate to the Father to some degree, thus maintaining the Father's sovereignty.

Since Tertullian and Novatian were labeled heretics for their moral rigorism, it is debatable what influence they had in later times. It is, however, a way of thinking that roughly corresponds to the outlined *logos* theology that also characterized Greek-speaking theologies in the first centuries. While this conception of God was far from unproblematic from the perspective of later trinitarian theology, early *logos* theology arguably had some advantages as it helped conceptualizing the biblical idea of God as hidden but revealed through the Word.

It does, however, raise the question whether God in reality stays at a distance? God the Father is the "monarch" (sole cause or principle) who reigns over the universe. If, however, this means that the Son of God, the Word, is secondary to God, then perhaps we may learn something *about* God from the incarnate Word in Christ, but it stills seems that we only have an indirect fellowship with God in this way. God and the world are ordered in a fundamentally

41. Tertullian, *Against Praxeas* 8.7.

42. Hippolytus, *Against Noetus* 10.

43. Hippolytus, *Against Noetus* 6.

44. Novatian, *On the Trinity* 31.

hierarchical manner that makes it impossible for God to engage directly with humanity. This may also have a problematic impact on human relations if they are seen as modeled on God.

These are some of the issues that had to be dealt with in the theology of the fourth century. So-called "subordinationist" theology was eventually rejected—in favor of a much more egalitarian view of God and creation that simultaneously emphasized the distinction between the two. However, before we go any further with that discussion, we need to have a closer look at how things developed in the third century in the theology of the great Alexandrian theologians, Clement and Origen, who gradually laid the ground for a new way of thinking about God.

2

Divine Pedagogy

Salvation as Communion With God

Early Christian theology is fascinating for its diversity of thought. Nevertheless, as we have seen, there were some recurring themes. Early Christian theology developed in a largely polemical context, but it also made positive and creative use of the philosophical ideas of the time. We have already touched on the idea that God is distant and incomprehensible, yet present through his Word, the divine *logos*. The distance between God and the world does not mean that God is completely absent from the world—or that we exist independently of God. On the contrary, we have our life and being *from* and *in* God, as already Paul reportedly made clear (cf. Acts 17:27–28). In such classical ontology of participation, everything has its being from God who is being itself.

Salvation means coming to participate in God through Christ. Paul spoke readily about being "in" Christ (e.g., Rom 6:11). In early Christian theology, such participatory thinking was, however, largely understood in moral terms. Irenaeus, for example, explained that God's Word took part in the whole of human life so that all kinds of humans could learn from him and be reborn as God's children. The Word of God became human in order to "save all through himself," he writes.[1] This line of thought was picked up by the great Alexandrian theologians, Clement and Origen. The Word of God is understood as an educator and teacher who raises humans to salvation as they come to participate in God through Christ. In the following, we will take a closer look at what this means for trinitarian theology.

The question remains whether the Son of God is divine like God himself, or merely a subordinate who connects God with humans. While Clement and Origen to a large degree continued earlier *logos* theology, they contributed to developing a more nuanced understanding of the relationship between God the Father and the Son. Origen argued importantly that the Son was begotten from the Father with an "eternal birth."[2] The idea that the two presuppose each other would become a central argument in the trinitarian theology of the fourth century, as we will see. First, however, we need to take a few intermediate steps.

A Dream of the Truth

The theological tradition rooted in Philo of Alexandria appears again at the turn of the third century with Clement of Alexandria (c. 150 250). While there is a polemical tone, it is balanced by an openness to pagan culture. Clement borrows extensively from Greek poets and philosophers. Egyptian religion, Indian gymnosophists ("naked wise men") and Buddhist sages are also examples of pagans who have attained a level of wisdom. God, says Clement, has rained down bits of truth on pagans and barbarians who have "a dream of the truth."[3] The basic monotheistic idea that "God is one" takes a philosophical turn in Clement. If God is one, then God must be uncomposed and infinite, goes the argument, which may be taken from Plato's dialogue *Parmenides*. God cannot, for

1. Irenaeus, *Against Heresies* 2.22.4.
2. Origen, *On First Principles* 1.2.4–5.
3. Clement, *Exhortation to the Heathen* 5.64.1.

this reason, be captured by human concepts and definitions.[4] As the creator of everything, God is inaccessible to humans, but God makes himself comprehensible through his Word, which connects the unique God with the diversity of creation.

According to Clement, Plato also had an eye for the Trinity. In the dialogue *Timaeus*, the creator god is referred to as the Father who is the cause of all good. In one of his letters, Plato described how everything revolves around "the King of all," while "the second" revolves around "the second" and "the third" around "the third."[5] This admittedly sounds rather cryptic, but Clement explains that it must be understood as referring to what he calls "the Holy Triad." The "third" is the Holy Spirit, while the Son is the "second" by whom everything is created, according to the will of the Father.[6] So far so good, the philosophers have understood much, but what is special about Christianity is that we only really know God through revelation. The Word of God reveals God by becoming human in Jesus. The gospel is not just *about* Christ, but is Christ himself who, "by becoming Gospel," has broken through the mysterious silence and prophetic riddles of the past.[7]

God is distant by nature, Clement explains, but present with his "power," the Word of God, which has become human in Jesus.[8] There can be no knowledge of God without revelation. This is what Moses understood when he had to give up seeing God face to face on Mount Sinai. The knowledge of God is a gift of grace, says Clement, given by the Father through the Son. The "tree of life" in Genesis is an allegory for Christ. Through his incarnation, Christ has borne fruit and given life to those who have tasted God's grace: "It was not without the tree that he came to our knowledge," Clement writes poetically, "for our lives were hung upon it that we might believe."[9]

4. Clement, *Stromateis* 5.81.4.
5. Plato, *Timaeus* 41A; Plato, *Epistles* 2.312e.
6. Clement, *Stromateis* 5.103.1.
7. Clement, *Exhortation to the Greeks* 1.10.1.
8. Clement, *Stromateis* 2.5.4.
9. Clement, *Stromateis* 5.71.4–5.

Clement places particular emphasis on the pedagogical and intellectual elements of salvation. We have a share in life and incorruptibility as long as we have fellowship with God, he writes, but falling away from the knowledge of God leads to corruption and death.[10] Salvation means becoming a child of God by learning from God's Word. As created beings, we have no natural relationship with the creator. However, the greatest proof of God's goodness is that he still cares for us by making us his children.[11] Unlike the "Gnostic" movements that Clement distanced himself from, humans are not children of God by nature, but by learning from Jesus we become adopted as children of God. This is not just a matter of understanding the believer's relation to God in terms of late antique ideas of the father as the head of the family. God's Word, says Clement, is both father and mother to his children.[12] Adoption means an affinity and participation in God through Christ, not just submission.

Irenaeus had previously explained that the Word of God became human "so that by partaking of the Word humans might be adopted and become children of God."[13] Clement gives it a pedagogical twist, writing that "the Word of God became human so that you might learn from a human how humans can become God."[14] Paul described the Law of Moses in the Jewish Scriptures as a "guardian" to lead the Jews to Christ (Gal 3:24). According to Clement, pagan culture and philosophy had a similar function for other peoples. The Son of God, the divine *logos*, can be described as an instructor and teacher who disciplines and educates humans to salvation.[15] The Son of God, writes Clement, has shown his goodness by taking on "flesh that could suffer" in order to become lord of all. God cares for all humans, but salvation unfolds differently from person to person, and from people to people.

10. Clement, *Stromateis* 5.63.8.
11. Clement, *Stromateis* 2.74.1.
12. Clement, *Christ the Educator* 1.6.42.3.
13. Irenaeus, *Against Heresies* 3.19.
14. Clement, *Exhortation to the Greeks* 1.8.4.
15. Clement, *Stromateis* 7.6.5–6.

There is a universal outlook in this expressed in what is perhaps an Easter hymn that appears in Clement's *Exhortation to the Greeks*.[16] The Son of God is described as a kind of sun god who visits all humankind on his chariot of the sun:

> Light without slumber has come over all,
> and sunset has turned to sunrise.
>
> This was the goal of the new creation:
> For the sun of righteousness, who rides over all,
> reaches evenly around all humankind,
> like his Father, who makes his sun
> rise over all humans
> and wets them with the dew of truth.
>
> He has turned sunset into sunrise,
> and through the cross turned death into life.
> He has torn humanity from destruction,
> and lifted it up to the skies.
> He has planted the mortal in immortality,
> and brought earth to heaven.

The metaphor of Christ as light is not surprisingly prominent in a theology like Clement's that emphasizes enlightenment. However, the cross also plays a role, as the transition from death to life, so that humans can come to share in God's immortality. The universal must be supplemented by the particular, since it is only by coming to know God as revealed in Jesus that we become children of God.

Relations of Love

The biblical texts must be read as testimonies to the Word of God, the *logos*, that inspired them.[17] For example, Clement—like Irenaeus—can read the story of the Good Samaritan as a story about God's Word, who became human in Jesus in order to come to our

16. Clement, *Exhortation to the Greeks* 11.114.1–5.
17. Scripture is "the voice of the Lord." Clement, *Stromateis* 7.95.4–5.

rescue.[18] The Samaritans were a foreign people to the Jews, and this illustrates well that God is foreign to us, yet nevertheless comes to our aid. The Samaritan depicts Jesus, who, as Clement puts it, came with the "bandages of salvation," faith, hope and love, the greatest of which, as Paul writes, is love (1 Cor 13:13). The discerning Christian knows God in love.[19]

We know the Father through the Son, explains Clement, just as "truth is known by the truth."[20] In other words, the Father and the Son belong together. To know God is to share in the relationship of mutual love that exists between the Father and the Son.[21] "God is love," as we hear in First John (1 John 4:7). In Clement's explanation of what this means, perhaps surprisingly, the femininity of God comes into play: "God himself is love, and out of love he became feminine," he writes. God is father in his "ineffable being," says Clement, but in his care for us, God became mother when he "begot" his Son for our sake. In other words, love is reproductive by nature: "The fruit that love produces is love."[22] It was also out of love, writes Clement, that the Son of God voluntarily became human and shared in our experience of weakness so that we, in turn, might be raised up to his strength. God's love reproduces itself in the Word, which draws humans into the community of love.

This particular understanding of God's love as something relational seems to be a rather original re-elaboration of relationality compared to the philosophy of the day.[23] The "mutual relations of love" between God the Father and the Son are characterized by reciprocity and freedom rather than asymmetry and necessity.[24] It is all rather philosophical, but Clement ties his reflections to the biblical stories of Jesus and his disciples. When Jesus instituted the

18. Clement, *Rich Man's Salvation* 29.2–6. See Roukema, "Good Samaritan in Ancient Christianity," 72.

19. Clement, *Stromateis* 5.103.1.

20. Clement, *Stromateis* 5.1.3–4.

21. See Osborn, *Clement of Alexandria*, 256.

22. Clement, *Rich Man's Salvation* 37.2.

23. See Maspero, *Cappadocian Reshaping of Metaphysics*, 114–19.

24. Clement, *Christ the Educator* 1.8.71.3.

Lord's Supper, he left a new covenant by giving of his love, says Clement. We must now show that love to each other.[25] God's love unfolds in human relations in the Christian community. God created the world for universal fellowship, but this is only realized when humans become children of God by sharing in the "common Word" that is Christ.[26]

Such participation removes the many distinctions we make between people. For Clement, if the aim of creation is community, this means that we must share the goods of creation, just as men and women must be considered of equal value in marriage.[27] The mutual relations of love that exist between God and God's Word take on practical value when humans are adopted and included in the community. In other words, trinitarian theology is largely a practical and ethical matter that aims at describing how humans become children of God.

A Harmonious Triad

In the theology of the early church, it was a common belief that everything is in a way "contained" by God.[28] If the world is not formed by a prior matter that exists independently of God, then everything in the world must be entirely dependent on God. Nothing can exist outside of God, but everything has its being by participating in God. This ontology was developed in philosophical terms by early Christian theologians, and it became central to the influential Alexandrian theologian Origen (c. 185–253) in the third century. When God describes himself to Moses as "the One who is," this means that all that exists participates in God the Father, who "truly is."[29] God is good, and everything that exists

25. Clement, *Rich Man's Salvation* 37.3–5.

26. Clement, *Christ the Educator* 2.8. The idea of a "common logos" is Stoic.

27. Clement, *Christ the Educator* 2.10.3—11.2. Clement's approval of gender-neutral language also seems to be a function of the idea of virtue as participation in the common *logos*.

28. So-called *pan-en-theism*, not to be confused with *pan-theism*.

29. Origen, *On First Principles* 1.3.3–6. Cf. Septuagint's Exodus 3:14.

participates in God's goodness—in distinction to Gnosticism's notion of matter or the created world as something evil.

Jesus, according to the Gospels, had said that only God is good (Mark 10:18), but this should not be taken to mean that the world is evil.[30] It simply means that creation does not have an *inherent* goodness, but rather borrows its goodness, so to speak. When there is good in the world, it is because creation shares in the good that comes as a gift from God. Sin, on the other hand, is alienation from God, while evil must be understood as the absence of good. According to Origen, when the Gospel of John states that "nothing" was created without the Word of God (John 1:3), this means that "nothing," i.e., evil, was created without God. Evil is not created by God, but arises when creation is broken, so to speak, because of sin.[31] This is the basis for the notion of evil as "privation," which became prevalent in subsequent theology.

God works with his Word in the history of the world to lead humans to salvation. God's Word is the divine *logos*, the reason, wisdom and justice in which all thinking beings participate to some extent. Christians, however, have a special relationship with Christ through the Holy Spirit.[32] As with Clement, there is a clearly pedagogical element in salvation that touches on the relation of the particular to the universal.[33] God's Word has become human in order to set humans free from the historically conditioned traditions and norms that characterize all cultures and peoples. The goal is to learn to live according to God's universal law.[34] Christians constitute a new people who participate in God directly through God's Word. To "put on Christ," explains Origen, means to partake of the wisdom, righteousness, holiness and so on that characterize Christ.[35]

30. Origen, *On First Principles* 1.2.13.

31. Origen, *Commentary on John* 2.92–93. The so-called privation theory of evil is often attributed to Neo-Platonism, but is also found in Origen.

32. Origen, *On First Principles* 1.3.8.

33. See Jacobsen, *Christ—the Teacher of Salvation.*

34. Origen, *Contra Celsum* 8.72.

35. Origen, *Commentary on Romans* 9.35.34.

Since Origen's theology is quite complex, it can be difficult to get a grip on the relationship between God and God's Word and how exactly this relationship is thought of in trinitarian terms. To a large extent, it must be seen in relation to salvation. This is clear from Origen's main theological work, *On First Principles*. Here Origen explains that in order for someone to be reborn by God, the Father, the Son and the Holy Spirit must all be present. As thinking beings, we all participate in the Father and the Word of God, but to become holy, we must also partake of the Holy Spirit.[36] In his commentary on Paul's epistle to the Romans, Origen explains that when Paul speaks of how God's "love has been poured out into our hearts" (Rom 5:5), he makes love the highest and greatest gift of the Holy Spirit.[37] It is with this gift, which God has first given us out of love, that we become capable of loving God. Once again, there is something trinitarian about the nature of love. God is called love, Origen notes, and so Christ is the Son of love, just as the Spirit is the Spirit of love. When the Holy Spirit pours love into our hearts, we become one in Christ and share in the nature of God (cf. 2 Pet 1:4).

Origen makes a clear distinction between God and God's Word, the *logos*, that has become human in Jesus. He does, however, also avoid separating the two completely. In his polemic against the Platonic philosopher Celsus, who had criticized the Christians, Origen denies that Christians worship multiple gods when they worship Christ.[38] The Son of God is one with God the Father, as Jesus makes clear when he says that "I and the Father are one" (John 10:30). Because of this oneness, says Origen, as Christians we worship one God—the Father and the Son. Jesus also calls himself "the truth," suggesting that Christ must also be eternal since truth has always existed. Christians worship "the Father of truth" and "the Son who is truth." Although they are two, they are one in unity of thought, harmony, and will. Christians believe in God through his

36. Origen, *On First Principles* 1.3.5–7.

37. Origen, *Commentary on Romans* 4.9.10.

38. Origen, *Against Celsus* 8.12.

Son, who is "Word, Wisdom, Truth, Justice," and whatever else we have learned to call the Son of God.[39]

There is not a multiplicity of gods, but Origen also makes it clear that we must avoid the opposite extreme, where the Father and the Son are not considered two independent realities but only aspects of God. Origen rejects the modalism (or Sabellianism) that Tertullian had already fought against. The Son of God is the Wisdom of God—the *Sophia* who speaks in the book of Proverbs (Prov 8:22).[40] To this degree, the Son of God has his own independent reality—or *hypostasis,* as it is called with a Greek term that would later become central to debates about the Trinity.

Origen also emphasizes, however, that there is an eternal relationship between the Father and the Son, who did not just come into being in the context of creation. The Father has never been without his Wisdom, which contains within itself the plan for all creation. Insofar as Wisdom communicates the plans and mysteries of God, it is called the Word of God, but it is also called the Son of God. If God is Father, then God must also have a Son.[41] The Son did not come into being in time, but the birth (or "generation") of the Son is eternal, it is outside of time. In other words, God is eternally the Father of the only-begotten Son through an "eternal birth"—or, using the metaphor of Christ as light, the Son is eternally begotten from the Father as "light is begotten of light."[42]

Is this "Subordinationism"?

The argument that the Father has always been the Father of the Son, who must have been begotten with an "eternal birth," would become central to subsequent Nicene theology. Fourth-century theologians argued that if the Father and the Son belong together eternally, the Son must be equally God. In Origen, however, it

39. Origen, *Against Celsus* 8.13.
40. Origen, *On First Principles* 1.2.1–3.
41. Origen, *On First Principles* 1.2.10.
42. Origen, *On First Principles* 1.2.4–5.

often sounds as if the Son of God is not divine in himself, but only has his divinity in a derived sense from God the Father. Origen explains that if the psalm about the king who is anointed (Ps 45) can be read as depicting Christ, it is because Christ was anointed with the Holy Spirit as a reward for his virtue and love for God.[43] However, Christ is more than just a human like others who have come to participate in God. When the psalm says that he was anointed "above" his equals (Ps 45:7), Origen explains, it means that the "essential fullness" of the Word of God was in him (cf. Col 2:9).[44]

This nevertheless raises the question whether the Son of God is divine by nature or only divine by participation in God the Father, who alone is divine in his own right? This, however, is perhaps a false dichotomy in the case of Origen. While only God the Father is without origin, the Son of God has no other beginning than God himself, says Origen.[45] For Origen, participation implies an intimate communion that is not, as in later theology, subject to the sharp distinction between the one who participates and the one who is participated in. The Son of God is divine *because* he fully participates in God.

The extent to which Origen understood the Son as subordinate to the Father is disputed.[46] In his commentary on the Gospel of John, he notes that the Savior is called "light," just as God is also called "light" in John's first letter.[47] This could be taken as a proof that the Son is not essentially different from the Father. However, says Origen, the two are not quite the same light because, while the Son is called the light that shines *in* the darkness (John 1:5), the Father is called the light in which there is *no* darkness (1 John 1:5). This indicates that the Father is light in a higher sense than the Son. That the Son is less than the Father must also be the point when Jesus says that "the Father is greater than I" (John 14:28).[48] Later theology

43. Origen, *Against Celsus* 1.56.

44. Origen, *On First Principles* 2.6.4.

45. See, e.g., Origen, *On First Principles* 1.2.9.

46. See Ramelli, "Origen's Anti-Subordinationism."

47. Origen, *Commentary on John* 2.149.

48. Origen, *Commentary on John* 13.151–53. Kinzig, *History of Early Christian Creeds*, 269.

often saw these words as referring only to Jesus's human nature or his relation to the Father in the economy of salvation, but this distinction was not fully developed before the fourth century.[49]

As was the case with the *logos* theology of the first centuries, Origen's theology is often described as a kind of *subordinationism*, where the Son is considered subordinate to the Father. While this may be true to some degree, it misses the mark since Origen also goes a long way to emphasize the eternal relationship between the Father and the Son. Before the fourth century, most (if not all) theologians considered the Son to be subordinate to the Father in one way or another.[50] Only in the trinitarian debates of the fourth century does it make sense to speak of "subordinationism" in the sense of a proper "doctrine."

To a large degree, Clement and Origen continued earlier theology. The Son of God is the divine *logos* that mediates between the distant God the Father and creation. They both contributed, however, to a relational understanding of God that would become central later on—even if it was only with extensive adjustments that we eventually arrived at what is now considered the "orthodox" or "classical" doctrine of the Trinity.

Origen's theology was influential in his own time and became the basis for theological discussions in the fourth century—regardless of theological orientation.[51] The debates on trinitarian theology were to a large degree a matter of deciding what to make of the Alexandrian legacy. In the following, we will take a closer look at the theological discussions that arose in the fourth century in connection with the Nicene Creed—discussions that led to wild and even violent conflicts and theological upheavals that resulted in the reformulation of the trinitarian theology of the early church.

49. See, e.g., Augustine, *On the Trinity* 1.7.14.

50. Hanson, *Search for the Christian Doctrine of God*, 64. Clement seems to have believed that Christ was subordinate to God the Father in his being. Clement, *Excerpts* 19.5; 33.2.

51. Ayres, *Nicea and Its Legacy*, 21.

3

"Same Being as the Father"

Nicene Theology and the Arian Controversy

The Council of Nicaea in AD 325 was a landmark event on more than one level—theologically and politically. Emperor Constantine (c. 285–337), who ruled from 306 to 337, had recently been more or less converted to Christianity. This proved significant for his policies, although he was not baptized until shortly before his death. While Christianity had previously been an often persecuted religion, it now came to play a central role in the Roman Empire. The church and the imperial power was gradually harmonized in a unified Christian culture. For this to work, there had to be agreement on the essential points of the order and practice of the church, as well as the basics of Christian doctrine.

Leading up to the Council of Nicaea, theologians had eagerly discussed important questions about the relationship between God the Father and God the Son. The Alexandrian priest Arius (c. 250–336) had made a name for himself by denying that the Son was eternal like the Father. He likely did so to defend what he saw to be the traditional belief in the oneness and monarchy of God the Father. However, according to his critics, Arius went too far by reducing the Son to a mere creature among others. This discussion gave rise to what is often called *the Arian controversy.*

Emperor Constantine initially convened the Council of Nicaea to streamline church practice and order, but it quickly became an opportunity to sort out theology as well. Perhaps around 300 bishops attended—according to a later anecdote including Nicholas of Myra (c. 280–345), also known as Santa Claus.[1] It was here that Nicholas allegedly slapped Arius when the latter denied Jesus's divinity. When Constantine grew tired of the skirmishes, he reportedly cut through and introduced the wording in the Creed stating that the Son of God has the "same being" as the Father—a formulation that became crucial to subsequent trinitarian theology.

Whether the story of Santa's assault on the "arch-heretic" Arius is true or not (it probably isn't!), it says something about the importance of the matter as perceived by later commentators. At stake was nothing less than our understanding of salvation, and as such, the gospel itself. The belief at the heart of the theology that unfolded in defense of the Nicene Creed was that Jesus can only save humans if he is fully God. However, it was only gradually that it became clear what should be understood by the central formulations of the creed. This is why we must also now delve into the theological discussions that followed in the years after Nicaea.

The Nicene Creed

In early theology before Nicaea, as described above, the Son of God was widely understood as a cosmic intermediary who connects us to an otherwise distant and inaccessible God. What is easily implied is that the Son of God cannot be God in quite the same way

1. The earliest known account of the story is from Petrus de Natalibus's *Catalogus sanctorum* from the fourteenth century. It should also be noted that Nicholas died around 345. The popular Christmas meme (at least in theological circles!) where a boy wants an uncomprehending Santa Claus to take a stand for *homoousion* or *homoiousion* fits poorly with the fact that the latter concept only became part of the discussion in the late 350s.

as God the Father. This, at any rate, was the conclusion reached by Arius, who claimed that only God the Father was truly God. The Son, on the other hand, was subordinate to the Father, he believed, and only "God" in a secondary or derived sense. As we have seen, this was a common line of thought, but Arius articulated his beliefs more sharply than had previously been done. The result was that he ended up in controversy with his bishop, Alexander, who eventually excluded Arius from the church in Alexandria. This, however, did not settle the case, as the controversy spread when it became clear that Arius was not alone in holding such views.

The polemic came to a temporary conclusion at the Council of Nicaea in 325. Here it was established that the Son of God is, as the Nicene Creed says, "of the being of the Father," "light of light," "true God of true God" and that the Son has the "same being" as the Father. In the context of the creed, the crucial phrases sound like this:

> We believe in one God, the Father Almighty, creator of all things visible and invisible.
>
> And in one Lord, Jesus Christ, the Son of God, begotten of the Father, only-begotten, that is, of the being of the Father, God of God, light of light, true God of true God, begotten, not made, the same being as the Father, by whom all things were made, both in heaven and on earth, who for us humans and for our salvation descended and became flesh and was made human, suffered and rose on the third day and ascended into heaven, from where he comes to judge the living and the dead.
>
> And in the Holy Spirit.[2]

It should be clear, then, that the Son of God is divine like his Father. If not, the Nicene Creed concludes with a series of condemnations of those—probably Arius and his friends—who claimed that the Son of God was "created out of nothing" and therefore has a being *other* than God. The latter should be understood in contrast to the view expressed in the creed that the Son of God is

2. The Greek text can be found in Kinzig, *History of Early Christian Creeds,* 246–48.

"of the being of the Father" and that the Son has the "same being" as the Father.[3] The latter became the prevailing view at the Council of Nicaea.

To modern ears, the Nicene Creed can sound rather poetic, but many of its formulations have philosophical underpinnings. It is difficult, however, to say exactly what those present at the council might have meant by the words. Perhaps the creed was based on a text written by the influential theologian and church historian Eusebius of Caesarea (c. 260–340), who was present in Nicaea.[4] The central statement saying that the Son of God has the "same being" as the Father was not his, however, and it was only with difficulty that he accepted the wording. Emperor Constantine seems to have found the theological discussion about the relationship between the Father and the Son rather unimportant or even silly, although he—or his advisor, the bishop Hosius of Cordoba (c. 259–359)—may have been behind the words that the Son has the "same being" as the Father.[5] What exactly was understood by this formulation is unclear, however, and perhaps it was only introduced to force agreement—and to get rid of Arius.

That the Son of God has the "same being"—in Greek *homoousios*—as the Father was a view that had previously been rejected at a church meeting in Antioch around 268. So it's not surprising if Arius and others were skeptical. At the time, the notion was associated with Sabellianism—the modalist theology that understood the Father and the Son as manifestations of one and the same divine person.[6] The notion that something could have the "same being" as God was also associated with forms of Gnosticism, where

3. In Greek *homoousios*, from *homo-*, same, and *ousios*, being.

4. At least according to Eusebius's own account, which might not, however, be very reliable. Eusebius, *Letter to His Church Concerning the Synod at Nicaea* 2–3. As Kinzig puts it, the Nicene Creed is not simply an extended version of Eusebius's text. Kinzig, *History of Early Christian Creeds*, 248.

5. Eusebius, *Letter to His Church Concerning the Synod at Nicaea* 4. Hosius is also known as Ossius.

6. See Hanson, *Search for the Christian Doctrine of God*, 190–202. Athanasius, *On the Councils of Ariminum and Seleucia* 43–45. Hilary, *On the Synods* 81–88.

creation was understood as emanation, a kind of outflow from the being of God. For many, there were materialistic undertones in speaking of God's "being," as if God was made of some stuff from which the Son of God was also formed. In this sense, it implied a division of God's being. This, however, is hardly how the term was understood by those who wrote the Nicene Creed.[7]

The word we translate as "being" (or "essence") is *ousia* in Greek, a word that comes from "to be." As such it was used in philosophy to refer to the essential nature of things. However, the term would gradually take on a new meaning in Nicene theology. Here it says less about God's essence or being in itself and more about the close relationship between God the Father and God the Son. That Christ has the "same being" as God the Father emphasizes that Christ is God—"God of God, light of light, true God of true God, begotten, not made," as the creed states. The Son of God has his being from God the Father, which is why he is also God.

We will have a much closer look at the discussions below, but first it should be clear what is *not* meant by the specific wording. When it is stated that the Son has the "same being" as the Father, it is hardly to be understood that the two are simply the same kind of things, as when we say, for example, that a bicycle and a car are both a kind of vehicle. This is clear when the creed says that the Son is "of the being of the Father" and that the Son is "begotten" (or "generated") by the Father. The Son has his being, so to speak, from the Father's own being and not from some generic God-stuff that precedes both the Father and the Son. The Son is begotten *of* the Father's being and therefore *has* the same being as his Father.[8]

It is especially the latter formulation about the "same being"—the concept *homoousios*—that would become disputed, but the notion must be understood in the light of the rest of the creed. While the discussion about the precise formulations may seem like technical details, it was connected to a larger theological

7. Nor is the Son "part" of the Father's being, but is *from* the Father. Eusebius, *Letter to His Church Concerning the Synod at Nicaea* 5–6.

8. This is why it might make sense to avoid the traditional translation of the Nicene Creed, which states that the Son is "*of* the same being" as the Father.

perspective concerning Jesus's identity as the Son of God and, ultimately, our understanding of salvation and the gospel. The specific formulations about the Son's being and relationship to the Father should be understood in light of what follows in the creed: how the Son became human "for us humans" and "for our salvation."

From the discussions that followed in the years after the Council of Nicaea, we can get a sense of what may have been meant by such formulations in the Nicene Creed—and if not, then at least how it came to be understood in subsequent theology. It is only gradually, however, that it becomes clear how important it is that the Son has the same being as the Father—and what far-reaching theological consequences it has that God must therefore be understood as triune. We'll come back to this below, but first we have to look at the initial debate in Alexandria about the relationship between God the Father and the Son.

Arius and Alexander

Since Emperor Constantine ordered Arius's books to be burned after the Council of Nicaea, it is not exactly clear what he believed and taught. However, we do know his views from a few letters and his critics. Athanasius quotes from Arius's *Thalia*—supposedly a song whose title means "cheerful," although the content is pretty heavy theology.[9] Its basic claim is that only God is without origin, but that the Son of God must have a beginning. This is how we get the formulation condemned at the end of the Nicene Creed that "there was a time when the Son was not." For the opponents, this was "Arianism" expressed in a nutshell, although it might not have expressed Arius's view very precisely. In a letter to his friend Eusebius of Nicomedia, he writes that the Son existed "before all time," but without being eternal like the Father.[10] The Son did not

9. Arius's *Thalia* is probably from around 322. Athanasius also quotes Arius's letter to Bishop Alexander. See Athanasius, *On the Councils of Ariminum and Seleucia* 15–16.

10. Arius, *Letter to Eusebius of Nicomedia*. According to Epiphanius, *Panarion* 69.6. The letter is probably from the year 318. See Hanson, *Search for the Christian Doctrine of God*, 6ff.

exist before he was created, but came into being before the creation of the world.

Arius, as mentioned, initially formulated his views against Alexander (c. 250–326), the bishop of Alexandria. As Arius saw it, the latter was guilty of Sabellianism, where the Father and the Son are only manifestations of God, but not individual persons. That God is one and simple was a common view at the time, but for Arius this meant that God the Father must be completely unique and as such essentially "foreign" to his Son.[11] This does not, however, mean that Arius rejected all notions of the Trinity, as he could also speak of a divine "triad." The debate was not, in other words, between an anti-trinitarian theology as opposed to an "orthodox" trinitarian one like the Nicene. The difference was that, according to Arius, there are degrees of dignity in the Trinity, since the Son of God is subordinate to God himself. There is no one equal to the ineffable God. Only the Father can be called "true God," since the Son of God only has his divinity in a derived and secondary sense.

This idea of God was linked to a specific understanding of creation. Arius seems to have believed that God first created his Son, who then helped create the rest of creation. As scriptural evidence for this view, one could—as mentioned above—point to the book of Proverbs in the Old Testament, where Wisdom seems to describe herself as having been made at the beginning of creation (Prov 8:22). It was common to understand Wisdom as identical with the Son of God, and so it was reasonable to conclude that the Son of God must have been created.[12] God produced his Son as a product of his "will and plan." This view may have its roots in Plato, who spoke of the creator who by an act of will creates and sustains the subordinate gods as part of the creation of the world.[13] Arius seems to be radicalizing this way of thinking. The

11. Arius's *Thalia* according to Athanasius, *On the Councils of Ariminum and Seleucia* 15.

12. Arius according to Athanasius, *Orations Against the Arians* 1.5. God may have his own uncreated Wisdom, but the Son of God participates in God's Wisdom as a secondary, created Wisdom. See also Hanson, *Search for the Christian Doctrine of God*, 6.

13. Plato, *Timaeus* 41.

Son is what he is only by virtue of God's will that is unbound and radically free. The wisdom of God is "radiance and light," but only exists by the will of God. The difference between the Father and the Son makes the Father incomprehensible to the Son, who does not even understand his own being.[14]

Alexander, the bishop of Alexandria, reacted to Arius's theology in a letter to another bishop named Alexander.[15] Here, he explains how Arius and his followers had sought out all the passages in the Scriptures that had to do with Christ's humiliation in the history of salvation in order to show that Christ could not be the unchangeable God. The humiliation and exaltation of Christ (Phil 2:6–9) was supposedly an argument that Christ must be changeable and only divine as a result of God's will, not by nature. According to Alexander, Arius and his followers claimed that God had foreseen before creation that Christ would do what was right, which is why he exalted Christ as the Son of God. Once again, the psalm about the king who is anointed because of his love for right is brought into play (Ps 45). This could be understood to mean that God has exalted Christ, who, according to Arius, cannot therefore be divine by nature, but has only become so in a derived sense by the will of God.[16]

However, it is a mistake to separate the Father and the Son in this way, argued Alexander, since the two are inseparable.[17] The Gospel of John speaks of "the only-begotten," who is "God himself," and who is "in the bosom of the Father" (John 1:18). Not even in our minds can we imagine any distance between them, argues Alexander. Creation was created out of nothing, he notes, it has a distance from God, but there can be no distance between the Father and the Son, since the two presuppose each other. The Father is always Father, but he can only be Father if the Son is

14. Athanasius, *On the Councils of Ariminum and Seleucia* 15; *Orations Against the Arians* 1.6.

15. Theodoret, *Ecclesiastical History* 1.3.

16. Alexander, *Letter to Alexander of Thessalonica* 3. Cf. Origen, *On First Principles* 2.6.4.

17. Alexander, *Letter to Alexander of Thessalonica* 3–4.

always with him.[18] God is incomprehensible in his being, all right, but that only means that the Father and the Son are both incomprehensible. When Paul speaks of Jesus as God's *own* Son (Rom 8:32), it is to distinguish him, who is by nature the Son of God, from humans, who are only called children of God in a figurative sense. If everything is created by the Son of God, he cannot himself have been created.[19] The fact that the Son of God is "begotten" of God is not the same as having been created or having come into being at a certain time, quite the contrary.[20] The Son is begotten of the Father, but this means that they are both God. In other words, their unity is not just moral, as Arius seems to have believed, but ontological, i.e., a matter of *being*.

This is roughly the theology encapsulated in the Nicene Creed. Unfortunately, the creed also condemned the view that the Father and the Son are distinct realities or persons in the sense of *hypostases* in Greek, which seems to have been Alexander's view—and in any case became the common view later on. Considered by these standards, it's not that the Nicene Creed hits the mark every time. There might also have been other ways of expressing the divinity of Christ than saying that the Son has the "same being" as the Father. As mentioned, there are indications that it was Hosius, Bishop of Cordoba in Spain, who, with the support of the emperor, pushed the formulation through—perhaps inspired by Tertullian's formulation of God as "one being cohering in three."[21] At any rate, the formulations in the Nicene Creed are probably best understood polemically. When it is said that the Son has the "same being" as the Father, this should not be taken as an attempt to define God's being with a philosophical concept. It only makes it

18. Alexander, *Letter to Alexander of Thessalonica* 7–8. Cf. Origen, *On First Principles* 1, 2, 4–5.

19. Alexander, *Letter to Alexander of Thessalonica* 6.

20. Alexander, *Letter to Alexander of Thessalonica* 11–12.

21. Hanson, *Search for the Christian Doctrine of God,* 190–202. That Latin already had a word for the Son having the "same being" as the Father is contradicted by the fact that the word *homoousios* remains untranslated in Latin versions of the Creed.

clear that the Son is *not* created, but that he is truly God—and that Arius and his friends were wrong.

Arius was far from alone in his theological beliefs. There are indications that he had his convictions from a theologian named Lucian of Antioch (c. 240–312), whose students now formed a more or less united front.[22] The bishop Eusebius of Nicomedia (died c. 342) and Asterius of Cappadocia (died c. 341) were among the main supporters of Arius. In many ways, they continued elements that already existed in the theological tradition. Rather than being the "arch-heretic" that tradition later made him out to be, Arius was a conservative theologian who read the Scriptures literally without too many exegetical workarounds.[23] The view that the Son was inferior and perhaps even essentially different from God himself was widespread, especially in the Greek-speaking, eastern part of the Roman Empire.

It was, as suggested above, only with hesitation that Eusebius of Caesarea signed the Nicene Creed. The Son existed "before all time," he believed, but without being eternal as the Father. Eusebius was a follower of Origen, and thus representative of a theological tradition that existed long before so-called "Arianism." In the traditional metaphor of God as light, the beam of a light-source cannot be separated from the source itself, but Eusebius explained that the Son must nevertheless be understood as having an independent reality different from the Father.[24] The Son is as such subordinate to the Father, who alone is God himself. Other theologians of the time held similar views—even within the established church. The Nicene Creed remained unacceptable to many of the bishops in the eastern part of the Roman Empire who followed this aspect of Origen's theology.[25] There was a hierarchy in which the Son of God was subordinate to God the Father.

22. Arius refers to Eusebius of Nicomedia as a "fellow Lucian." We may as such speak of "Lucians" rather than "Arians." See, e.g., Jenson, *Triune Identity*, 80–81.

23. Young, *From Nicea to Chalcedon*, 48.

24. Eusebius, *Proof of the Gospel* 5.1.

25. See Kinzig, *History of Early Christian Creeds*, 268–78.

Such views were not necessarily considered "Arian" by those who held them. At the so-called *Dedication Council*, held in connection with the consecration of a new church in Antioch in 341, the assembled bishops made it clear that they were not disciples of Arius—after all, he was just a priest—but they did avoid the central Nicene formulations about God's "being." Instead, the Son of God is described as an "image" of the Father. This was the beginning of a series of councils that still more explicitly rejected Nicene theology. The Latin Western church largely adhered to the Nicene Creed, but in the Eastern church the view gained ground that we must avoid talking about God's being—and instead just talk about the Son as *similar* to the Father.[26] In other words, the case was far from settled.

The Word of God—"For Us"

For the first few decades after the Council of Nicaea, theological discussions were relatively calm. Only after the death of Emperor Constantine in 337 did the disputes over the Nicene Creed flare up again. Changing emperors fought for power in the Roman Empire, and the turmoil left its mark on theology. Athanasius of Alexandria (c. 296–373) had attended the Council of Nicaea in 325 as secretary to Bishop Alexander. He soon became a bishop himself and one of the most important champions of the theology that was understood to underlie the Nicene Creed. This was first expressed in three polemical speeches against the "Arians" from the early 340s—long after Arius, who died in 336, had originally put forward his views.[27]

When Athanasius talks about the "Arians," it is a collective, polemical term for all—especially Arius, Asterius and Eusebius of Nicomedia—who considered the Son of God to be created or to some degree subordinate to the Father. He can even call his

26. So-called *homoian* theology as opposed to Nicene *homoousian* theology.

27. Traditionally there are said to be four speeches, but the fourth is hardly by Athanasius.

opponents "Ariomaniacs," i.e., crazy Arians, with whom he was clearly rather annoyed. Athanasius reports how the Arians went around the city's marketplaces and recruited people, approaching young men and women with arguments to show that the Son of God could not be truly God.[28] Regardless of whether this account is accurate or not, it suggests that the discussion was not reserved for theologians. The Arian arguments came from everyday human experience. Just as a woman's child only comes into being at birth, the Son of God must also have come into being at some point, they argued. This may seem reasonable, but according to Athanasius, it was a mistake to try to understand the relations between God the Father and the Son in terms of human relations.

"God does not make humans his measure," Athanasius states. Only in God is there a complete father-son relationship, after which all human father-son relationships are named (cf. Eph 6:6).[29] However, we know enough from human relations that our offspring have exactly the same human being as ourselves.[30] If, after all, we are to understand God's father-son relationship on the basis of human relations, then this is the point we can take away, and not that God's Son is created. That the Son of God in the Nicene Creed is "begotten, not made" should be understood in contrast to creation, which is not born of God. We may talk of God as the "unoriginate" creator of things created and made. However, such a theology of creation will not get us far. It is better to speak of God as Father in relation to the Son.[31] We know the Father through the Son and vice versa, since the two presuppose each other, as also Alexander (and Origen before him) had pointed out.[32]

28. Athanasius, *Orations Against the Arians* 1.22.

29. Athanasius, *Orations Against the Arians* 1.23.

30. Athanasius, *Orations Against the Arians* 1.26.

31. Athanasius, *Orations Against the Arians* 1.33–34. That God the Father is "unoriginate" in contrast to creation cannot be used as an argument that the Son is created. The Son is begotten, not originated like creatures.

32. Athanasius, *Orations Against the Arians* 2.78; 2.81–82. See chapter 2 on Origen.

It is part of the Father's nature to be good, Athanasius explains, just as it is part of his nature to beget the Son.[33] The Son of God did not come into being as a result of the Father's will or decision, as Arius seems to have believed, but is eternal like the Father. When the Scriptures say that the Son of God has "become" something, this only refers to what God has become *for us* in the history of salvation. In himself, God is inaccessible to humans, Athanasius explains, but out of love for humans, the Word of God becomes what humans need.[34] When the Word became flesh to bring salvation to all, he "became" salvation for us, just as he also became life, propitiation and resurrection.

When Sophia says in the Septuagint translation of the book of Proverbs that "The Lord made me the beginning of his ways for his works" (Prov 8:22), this does not mean that Wisdom is a creature. Rather, argues Athanasius, it means that God has created a beginning *for* Wisdom.[35] The Son of God, who is Wisdom, is eternal, but has been given a beginning for the sake of creation. This happened when "the Word became flesh and made his dwelling among us," as it says in the Gospel of John (John 1:14).[36] When, however, Wisdom says that "before the mountains were settled, and before all hills, he begets me" (Prov 8:25), *this* can be taken to refer to Christ as the eternal Son of God, since it talks about the begetting, but not the creation, of the Son. The Son *as* God is not, then, an intermediary between God and creation, but only *becomes* so in the incarnation.

Athanasius makes a shift in the interpretation of the psalm about the king who is anointed by God (Ps 45). In earlier theology, as described above, this was often understood allegorically in such a way that the Son of God—the king—had been given a share in

33. Athanasius, *Orations Against the Arians* 3.66.

34. Athanasius, *Orations Against the Arians* 1.63–64.

35. Athanasius, *Orations Against the Arians* 2.44. Hanson calls this a "ridiculously far-fetched interpretation," although it does express a new, revolutionary idea of the Trinity that was "entirely consonant with Scripture." Hanson, *Search for the Christian Doctrine of God*, 424.

36. Athanasius, *Orations Against the Arians* 2.47.

God through the Holy Spirit before the creation of the world. This is now taken to refer to God's relationship with humanity through Christ. When the psalm speaks of the anointing of the king as an event, it could, according the "Arian" logic, be understood that Christ only has his divinity from God in a secondary sense and not by nature. However, Athanasius's point is that Christ, *as* a human, is not anointed for his own sake, but for the sake of humanity.[37] Christ is anointed in our place, he argues, it is we who are anointed in him.

God is "one deity in a triad," writes Athanasius.[38] While this seems to be a quite clear definition of the Trinity, he is more interested in what it means for how we read the Bible than in abstract theories about how something can be one and three at the same time. Nicene theology implies a particular view of Scripture, an approach to the Bible that is to be read in accordance with what is sometimes called a *partitive exegesis*. We must read Scripture as a double testimony to the Savior, Athanasius explains: some passages testify to him as the eternal God, while others say something about what he has become for us when he became human.[39] For example, when the Bible says that the Son of God is *given* something by God, it refers to what he receives as a human on our behalf.[40] As humans, we tend to lose what we receive, but for God's grace to be inalienable, God himself must receive it on humanity's behalf, as a human—which is why Jesus must be God if he is to save humans.[41]

It is remarkable how little the specific wording of the Nicene Creed is used in Athanasius's works against the Arians. Only in a treatise on the Nicene Creed from around 353 does he begin to defend the precise wording of the creed. Athanasius admits that the somewhat philosophical formulations about God's "being" are not biblical. However, they were necessary to make it clear that the Son is divine as the Father. By saying that the Son is "of the being

37. Athanasius, *Orations Against the Arians* 1.46.
38. Athanasius, *Orations Against the Arians* 3.15.
39. Athanasius, *Orations Against the Arians* 3.29.
40. Athanasius, *Orations Against the Arians* 3.40.
41. Athanasius, *Orations Against the Arians* 3.38.

of the Father" and that the Son has the "same being" as the Father, the authors of the Nicene Creed clearly rejected any notion that the Son was "created" and "changeable" and that he did not exist until he was "begotten" of God.[42]

It is not enough to say that the Son is *similar* to the Father, as some theologians would do.[43] Such similarity could be taken to mean that the Son is an image of the Father, but that the two are different in nature or being. For Athanasius, this was a subtle way of reintroducing Arianism—a suspicion reinforced by the subordinationism present in a number of creeds from the 350s. It is more accurate to say that the two are not just similar, but that they have a similar *being*. This was suggested by Basil of Ancyra (died c. 364) and others in an attempt to find a moderate middle ground between Nicene theology and its detractors.[44] While not completely hostile to this argument, for Athanasius it was better to stick to the Nicene formulation that the Son has the *same* (not just *similar*) being as the Father. Doing so makes it clear that the Son of God really *is* God.

Once again, these are not just theoretical quibbles, since humanity's relationship with God is at stake. It is, Athanasius explains, only because the Son of God is truly God that he can make humans participate in God. Everything created shares in God's grace through participation and can therefore resemble God to some extent, but the Son of God is God in his being.[45] Once again, the Word of God is not just a mediator in a cosmic hierarchy, but the eternal God who for our salvation has become human in Jesus Christ *for us*. This was the point of Nicene theology.

42. Athanasius, *On the Council of Nicaea* 20.

43. The Son is *homoios*, i.e., "like" the Father, at least in some respects, which, however, may not be incompatible with the idea that the Son is essentially unlike the Father in his *being*. See Hanson, *Search for the Christian Doctrine of God*, 557–79.

44. The view was possibly put forward in the lost Third Sirmian Creed of 358. The Son is *homoiousios* with the Father, rather than *homoousios*.

45. Athanasius, *On the Councils of Ariminum and Seleucia* 51.1–2.

Believe, Understand, Worship

In addition to the creed, the Council of Nicaea also adopted a number of regulations for organizing the church. For Emperor Constantine, establishing a common date for the celebration of Easter was probably more important than sorting out theological details. As evidenced by his letter to Arius and Alexander, he found it difficult to see the point of the discussion about the relationship between the Father and the Son.[46] The decisions at Nicaea were, to this degree, more about political-religious unity than about theology proper. However, while the political motive seems to be clear enough, we must nevertheless avoid the anachronistic view that religion was merely instrumentalized for political purposes. The modern distinction between religion and politics was unknown then. For the emperor, religious unity was necessary to secure God's favor and in this way to secure political unity.

After a few years, Constantine attempted to reinstate Arius in the church to settle things. Athanasius, on the other hand, was exiled several times from the 330s onwards, probably mostly due to his harsh treatment of his church-political opponents, the Meletians. There are indications that Constantine himself held Arian views—paradoxically enough, considering his involvement in Nicaea. But after all, Arian theology—or other forms of subordinationism—seems best suited for justifying earthly political power through political theology. With God the Father as the "monarch" at the top of a hierarchically ordered reality, the one rule of the emperor could be seen as corresponding to the one God in heaven, as Eusebius of Caesarea argued.[47] In contrast, Nicene theology seems to exclude such a political theology with its egalitarian view of God.[48] In any case, when Constantine was baptized just before

46. Constantine according to Eusebius, *Life of Constantine* 2.64–72.

47. See Eusebius, *Oration in Praise of Constantine* 3; Eusebius, *Life of Constantine* 2.19.

48. The emperor may have played a pivotal role in establishing Nicene orthodoxy, but its logic would eventually undermine the attempt to formulate a hierarchical political theology based on a subordinationist view of God. This was the point famously made by Erik Peterson. See Peterson, "Monotheism as a Political Problem," 94–96; 104.

his death in 337, this was administered by Eusebius of Nicomedia, whose theology in many ways resembled Arius's subordinationism.

Things didn't get any better when Constantine's descendants came to power after his death in 337. The Roman Empire was divided in two, but from 350 Constantius II (c. 317–61) was the sole ruler. In an attempt to settle disputes, he called a series of church meetings in Sirmium (in present-day Serbia). This led to more explicit rejections of the Nicene legacy, culminating in the Third Council of Sirmium in 357, which explicitly rejected the central formulations about the being of God in the Nicene Creed. The Greek translation of Isaiah rhetorically asks, "who shall declare his generation?" (Isa 53:8), and this was taken to refer to the begetting of the Son from the Father. The answer, many believed, was that no one can, and that we should, for this reason, refrain from saying anything about the "being" of the Father and the Son. The subordinationism of the Second Sirmian Creed is clear, however, when it states that "the Father is greater than the Son in honor and glory."[49] The creed was called "the Sirmian blasphemy" by opponents. Notable among the signatories was Hosius of Cordoba, Constantine's advisor, who had been known as a follower of Nicene orthodoxy, but was now probably forced to sign.[50]

Athanasius was later nicknamed "against the world" (*contra mundum* in Latin). For a time it seemed that he was alone in his defense of Nicene theology. However, there were other theologians who defended the Nicene Creed. From the West, the Latin theologian Hilary of Poitiers (c. 315–367) came to play a part in defending Athanasius. Hilary was bishop of Gaul, but from 356 to 360 he was exiled to Phrygia in the Eastern Roman Empire, possibly because of his reluctance to sign a series of condemnations against Athanasius. It was in this connection that he became aware of the details of the discussions about the Nicene Creed. As a result, Nicene theology also became part of the intellectual landscape in Latin speaking theology.

49. Kinzig, *History of Early Christian Creeds*, 299–302.

50. Athanasius, *History of the Arians* 45.4. Hanson, *Search for the Christian Doctrine of God*, 336.

Hilary emphasized the incomprehensibility of God more than Athanasius did. As the creator of all things, God the Father is beyond human reach. God is infinite and inaccessible to limited beings. Something similar was also argued by the Arians, but to Hilary it did not mean that the Son does not know the Father, as Arius had claimed. On the contrary, it is precisely through the Son that we know the Father, since no one knows the Father *except* the Son (Matt 11:27). In his main work on the Trinity, Hilary, for this reason, encourages his readers to "let our thoughts of the Father be at one with the thoughts of the Son." Due to the limitations of language, our confession of God will always be incomplete. The perfect knowledge of God consists in a kind of knowledge that is conscious of its own ignorance, says Hilary: we must believe, understand and worship, so that "acts of devotion" take the place of definitions.[51] In other words, the Nicene belief that the Son of God has the "same being" as the Father is not a philosophical "theory" about the nature of God, but a way of *doing* theology. It spells out the basic grammar of trinitarian theology, so to speak.

Perhaps the argument can be summarized by saying that we know God only as triune, but not as a philosophical definition. The Son of God did not become human in order for us to conceptualize God as creator, writes Hilary, but so that we could come to know God as the Father of the Son who speaks to us in Christ.[52] If we want to speak in philosophical and abstract terms about God, there are limits to how far we can go with our concepts. This realization should, as theologian T. F. Torrance has pointed out, remind us that Nicene theology must at its core be understood in its ecclesial context. It is only by the intimate communion with God in Christ through the Spirit that human reason becomes adapted to knowing God.[53] Theology presupposes the tradition and practice of the church in its talk about God. This does not mean that

51. Hilary, *On the Trinity* 2.6–7.

52. Hilary, *On the Trinity* 3.22.

53. Torrance, *Trinitarian Faith,* 56. Cf. Zizioulas, *Being as Communion,* 117–18. Dogmas are not rational definitions of God, but signs of the communion with God in which the church participates.

theology is a matter of uncritically accepting old dogmas—after all, Nicene theology was quite revolutionary in many respects, as we have seen. It only means that theology cannot be done without some recourse to tradition and the church in the broad ecumenical sense.

In a larger perspective, this means that Christianity cannot just talk in general religious terms about God as creator and then only subsequently talk about Jesus and all that is more specifically related to the Christian faith. For this reason, we should also be careful not to distinguish too sharply between the parts or articles in creeds like the Nicene. We do not begin with a detached concept of God as creator and only then add Jesus afterwards. The Son of God, who became human in Jesus, is part of the story from the beginning and must be understood as implied when we speak of God the Father as almighty creator—which is, of course, also evident when the creed says that "all things" were created by the Son of God. Where the Father is, there is also his Word, writes Athanasius.[54] The Christian faith hinges on the triune God, and that is where we must begin when we think and speak theologically.

54. Athanasius, *On the Council of Nicaea* 11.

4

Unity in Diversity

The Trinity in Cappadocian Theology

THEOLOGICAL DISPUTES IN THE fourth century were very much a political issue. This is evident from the numerous councils and new creeds from the mid-fourth century. That politics had become involved only made discussions about the Trinity more complex as theological formulations had to be carefully balanced by diplomatic considerations. Nicene theology was increasingly challenged by theologies that claimed, to varying degrees, that the Son of God was subordinate to the Father. Arius was long dead and buried, but there was still widespread skepticism about the Nicene belief that the Son of God has the *same being* as his Father. Many would eventually agree on rejecting the Nicene Creed, but there was no clear consensus on what to put in its place.

Some theologians had tried to find a middle ground where the Son could be said to be *similar in being* to the Father. This was now denied by two priests, Aetius (died c. 367) and Eunomius of Cyzicus (died c. 393), who from the 360s came to represent a new, radical opposition to Nicene theology, so-called Neo-Arianism. This gave rise to new discussions, just as new political-religious front lines were formed after the death of Emperor Constantius II in 361. Emperor Julian "the Apostate" (c. 332–363) managed in his short reign from 361 to 363 to completely reject Christianity in favor of a kind of syncretistic Neo-Platonism. Perhaps this is why he was friendly towards Aetius, who had argued against Athanasius that God could not possibly have been born of a woman.[1] Julian's successor Jovian was a follower of Nicene Christianity, but was replaced after only one year by Valens (328–378), who favored a theological line that avoided discussions about the being or nature of God, while seeing the Son as somewhat subordinate to the Father.[2] Only when Valens was replaced by Theodosius I (347–395) in 378 did Nicene theology finally come back into favor.

It is in this context that we encounter the siblings Macrina the Younger, Basil of Caesarea and Gregory of Nyssa, and their companion Gregory of Nazianzus, who carried out much of their work in Cappadocia in present-day Turkey. These "Cappadocians"[3] helped to give Nicene theology the form that was ratified at the Council of Constantinople in 381. Central to this is the distinction between the *being* and *persons* of God. As in Nicene theology, the Father and the Son go together, but Cappadocian theology developed a more nuanced understanding of the relation between the common and the particular. The Cappadocians further developed the relational understanding of God, in a way that would eventually leave a mark beyond theology proper—not least in the view of human relations.

1. See Hanson, *Search for the Christian Doctrine of God*, 604.

2. So-called *homoian* Arianism. Valens, however, hardly considered himself an "Arian," but favored what he perceived as a moderate middle way. Kahlos, "Misunderstood Emperor?," 61–78.

3. There were other theologians in Cappadocia—including Eunomius(!)—but the term is traditionally applied to Basil and the Gregories, while Macrina is now often also included.

How to Talk About God

Cappadocian theology largely took shape in confrontation with the so-called Neo-Arians, the priests Aetius and Eunomius.[4] Aristotelian philosophy seems to have undergone a renaissance at the time, and this was reflected in the two priests' attempt to place theology on a rational, logical footing. They combined this approach with a Platonic understanding of language, in which concepts were derived from the nature of things. Whereas Arius had originally described God as ineffable and incomprehensible, even to the Son of God, the idea was now that theological language corresponds to the nature of God. Whereas previous rejections of the Nicene Creed had been based on a skepticism against saying anything about the nature or being of God, what now prevailed was what may be described as a kind of theological rationalism.

The argument of Aetius and Eunomius was, in short, that all our concepts of God boil down to God being "unbegotten" by nature. Previous theologians had also emphasized that God the Father is unbegotten, but for Aetius and Eunomius it became the principle of theology. That God is unbegotten is simply what makes God unique. However, this was also why the Son of God could not have the same being as God the Father. If God is by definition unbegotten, Aetius claimed, then God cannot be born of a woman without ceasing to be God. The Son of God is by definition "begotten" but cannot, for this reason, have the same nature or being as the unbegotten God the Father.[5] Eunomius in a similar vein rejected the Nicene Creed's metaphor for the Son of God as "light of light" and the notion of the eternal birth of the Son.[6] Christ could not possibly be divine in the same way as God himself. The "rationalism" of this way of thinking lies in the attempt to define and capture the being of God in the words we use about

4. Eunomius quotes Arius's creed, according to Basil, *Against Eunomius* 1,4. If Eunomius saw himself as Arius's successor, it makes sense to refer to him as a Neo-Arian.

5. Aetius according to Epihanius, *Panarion* 76.6.1.

6. Eunomius according to Basil, *Against Eunomius* 2.1. Hanson, *Search for the Christian Doctrine of God*, 633; 620.

God, instead of seeing our theological language as limited and provisional.

For those who wanted to defend Nicene orthodoxy, this made it necessary to reconsider what it even means to do theology and talk about God. Basil of Caesarea (c. 330–379) was originally of the opinion that the Son is *similar in being* to the Father, but that we should be careful not to talk about them having the *same being*—a view he shared with his namesake Basil of Ancyra and others, as described above.[7] This view does not explicitly exclude the Nicene understanding that the Son has the same being as the Father, but it's a more cautious approach than the original Nicene understanding. However, both views came under fire when the Neo-Arians completely rejected that the Son is similar in being to the Father, let alone that the Son has the same being as the Father.[8] It was this radical rejection of Nicene theology that made it necessary to think things through anew.

Basil, in his dispute with Eunomius, formulated the notion that our language about God is in a way "conceptual."[9] That is, we continually invent language to describe God as we get to know God, but our concepts do not comprehend the being or nature of things. When we talk about the being of something, we are dealing with what is common to what is described. When we talk about individual things, we are talking about the properties particular to each individual. The same is true of God. When we talk about the being of God, we are dealing with what is common to the Father, the Son, and the Spirit. If, however, we speak specifically about the Father and the Son as distinct persons, we are talking about what is particular to each of them.[10] The Father and the Son are

7. So-called *homoiousians* believed that the Son is *similar in being* to the Father, but not necessarily that the Son has *the same being* as the Father, as the Nicene *homoousians* argued.

8. Neo-Arians are also described as *heteroousians*, i.e., someone who considers the being of the Son to be *different* from that of the Father, or the more misleading *anhomoian* (or *anomeans*), i.e., someone who claims that there is no similarity *at all* between the Father and the Son.

9. Or *epinoetic* to use the Greek term. Basil, *Against Eunomius* 1.5.

10. Basil, *Letters* 214.2–4.

two distinct persons, but with one common being. The one may be "unbegotten," while the other is "begotten," but this does not mean that they do not have the same being.

There are several philosophical and conceptual details at play when trying to understand what is meant by a "person." The word comes from the Latin word for mask, but in trinitarian theology we typically use the Greek word *hypostasis*, which denotes a more independent, underlying reality. In the condemnations that followed the Nicene Creed, the notion that the Son of God was "of a different hypostasis" from the Father was rejected. For the critics of Nicene theology, this rejection was dangerously close to the view that God is only one person who manifests himself in different ways, i.e., "modalism" or Sabellianism. In pre-Cappadocian theology, the philosophical concept of *hypostasis* was often used as a synonym for the nature or being of things. Origen, as noted, had described the Father, Son, and Holy Spirit as three independent *hypostases*, while Arius apparently claimed that the Son of God in "his hypostasis" has "nothing of God's own," which was why they could not have the same being.[11] Contemporary Neo-Platonism also talked about reality as in three *hypostases*, but these were not characterized by equal or mutual relations as would become the case in Cappadocian theology.

Since *hypostasis* and *being* (*ousia* in Greek) were understood more or less synonymously, it was no wonder that the notion of multiple divine *hypostases* was rejected by Nicene theologians. Gradually, however, it became clear that we need to distinguish between God's persons as related on the one hand and God's simple being on the other. Athanasius had already accepted that there might be some reason to distinguish between being and *hypostasis*.[12] In Cappadocian theology, the universal and collective aspects of Nicene theology is balanced by an increasing awareness of the individual person.[13] Two individuals can have the same being, yet

11. Origen, *Against Celsus* 8.12; Arius's *Thalia* according to Athanasius, *On the Councils of Ariminum and Seleucia* 15.

12. Athanasius, *Synodal Letter to the People of Antioch* 6.

13. Central to this is a letter, *Letter* 38, traditionally attributed to Basil, but more likely written by Gregory of Nyssa.

be distinct persons—*hypostases*—that relate to each other. That the divine persons have the same being is demonstrated by the inseparability of their activities. The Father is "unbegotten light," writes Basil, the Son is "begotten light," but both are light as in the traditional Nicene metaphor of the Son of God as "light of light."[14] Their communion points back to a common being—but without making it possible to define the being of God independently of relations as attempted by the Neo-Arians.

When we speak of the divine persons having the "same being," it is, says Basil, a way of saying that God's community is without distance.[15] The being of God, it seems, must be understood from the communion of persons rather than the other way around. Scholars, such as Greek Orthodox theologian John Zizioulas, have famously argued that Cappadocian theology thus makes personhood the fundamental principle of being.[16] The divine persons are not products of an abstract divine being, but the *person* of God the Father is the origin of the Son and the Holy Spirit. It would probably be an exaggeration to call this *personalism* in the modern sense, but God's personal relations cannot be avoided in talking about God. If we reject the kind of theological rationalism that seeks to define God's being in the abstract, we will have to speak of God in relational and personal terms instead.

In Cappadocian theology in general, there is a strong skepticism against defining the nature or being of things. In a letter, Basil makes it clear that since we do not understand the physiology of even the minutest ant, we must refrain from boasting about our knowledge of "the things that are." It was, as Basil saw it, just that—boasting—that Eunomius had done in his attempt to define the nature of God.[17] If we want to talk about God, we must content ourselves with

14. Basil, *Against Eunomius* 1.20; 2.25; 3.1. Hanson, *Search for the Christian Doctrine of God*, 689.

15. Basil, *Of the Holy Spirit* 18; 68.

16. God's being *is* simply communion, Zizioulas argued. Zizioulas, *Being as Communion*, 134. Zizioulas, *Being as Communion*, 89. Cf. Maspero, *Cappadocian Reshaping of Metaphysics*, 4–17.

17. Basil, *Letters* 16.1.

describing the divine persons in their relations and activities. These were the arguments that became decisive in the defense of Nicene theology up to the Council of Constantinople in 381.

A Time to Be Silent—and a Time to Speak

The line of thinking described above is echoed in Gregory of Nyssa (c. 335–395), famous for his "negative theology" developed in defense of the Nicene understanding of the Trinity.[18] If we want to talk about the being or nature of God, we must content ourselves with saying something about what God is *not*, hence the "negative." If we want to say something about what God actually is, however, we cannot avoid talking about God in trinitarian terms. This is laid out in detail when Gregory begins his polemical works against Eunomius after the death of his older brother Basil in 379.

When we speak of God the Father, we have implicitly said something about the Son of God, Gregory explains to dispel the misconception that the two can be separated. This is the traditional argument that goes back to Origen, Alexander and Athanasius. We cannot have any detached concept of God as Father. When someone believes in the Father "at the command of the Lord," Gregory writes, they "receive the Son together with him in their thoughts."[19] The two are intimately connected, so the mind wanders from the Son to the Father without having to jump over an "intermediate gap." On the other hand, when, like Eunomius, one stares blindly at the term "unbegotten" for God, one gets at most an abstract or "naked" conception of God by having failed to take Christ into account.

This, as we know from Nicene theology, is because the Son eternally belongs with the Father, which was the point in saying that the Son is "light of light," but also, says Gregory, "life of life" and so on.[20] There is a radical distance—or gap—between God and

18. See Steenbuch, *Negative Theology*, 25–32.

19. Gregory of Nyssa, *Refutation of the Confession of Eunomius* 100.

20. Gregory of Nyssa, *Against Eunomius* 1.1.688.

creation, but there is no distance between the persons of God, who are equal. Gregory, for this reason, also rejected Eunomius's claim that the Son is made to "obey" the Father. It is only when Christ came "in the form of a servant" that he became obedient (Phil 2:7–8), but obedience is not in his nature as such. Not even in his passion was the "king of glory" separated from his authority, and so we must reject any idea of his subordination to another authority.[21]

The relational understanding of love that first appeared in Clement of Alexandria is developed further by Gregory of Nyssa in his polemics against Eunomius.[22] The relationship between the Father and the Son is not an unequal relationship between separate individuals, but a mutual relationship between persons with the same divine being. The infinity and simplicity of God is central to the argument.[23] Since the being of God is infinite and simple, it cannot be divided, Gregory argues. Simplicity so understood does not, however, entail singularity, but makes possible an understanding of God as the unity of mutually related persons. Even though Jesus can say that "only one is good" (Matt 19:17), this does not mean that the Son only shares in the Father's goodness by participation, but rather that the Son is good in his being because the Son has the same being as the Father. This also means that relations are not just something accidental to things, but that relations can now be understood as inherent to being. Far-reaching philosophical conclusions may be drawn from this as we can now perhaps even talk of a "relational ontology."[24] However, the fundamentally anti-rationalist thrust of the argument should be kept in mind, as Gregory continues to emphasize the limits of human reason. The purpose was to safeguard the basic truths of trinitarian theology.

Gregory attended the Council of Constantinople in 381, but seems to have been rather weary of what he depicted as the constant Neo-Arian chatter in the city. This is expressed when he famously tells the story of how he could barely exchange money or buy a loaf

21. Gregory of Nyssa, *Refutation of the Confession of Eunomius* 142.

22. E.g., Gregory of Nyssa, *Against Eunomius* 1.337.1—1.338.1.

23. Gregory of Nyssa, *Against Eunomius* 3.9.20–21.

24. See Maspero, *Cappadocian Reshaping of Metaphysics*, 140–55.

of bread without being showered with claims that "the Father is greater than the Son."[25] Just as Athanasius reported how the Arians went around the marketplaces with theological propaganda, Neo-Arianism was also widespread among the people, if we are to believe Gregory's testimony. Of course, perhaps we shouldn't, since what seems to be most of all a rhetorical maneuver arguably says more about the elitist nature of Nicene and Cappadocian theology—in distinction to Neo-Arianism, which was seen as a more simple-minded approach to theology. Cappadocian theologians, similar to Clement and Origen, emphasized the allegorical and spiritual meaning of Scripture, which required contemplation and education, while the simpler and less careful arguments had to be rejected.

Gregory joined his brother Basil in emphasizing that all language is interpretive or "hermeneutic."[26] This is true for theological language as well as everyday language. Like his brother, Gregory displays a fundamental skepticism towards philosophical attempts at defining the being of things. Creation understands neither God nor itself. The language of theology does not capture God's incomprehensible being, as Eunomius believed. Theological language is conceptual, it is invented as we think about God. For example, says Gregory, when we call God merciful, it is not an abstract description of God's being, but of the good that God has done in the history of salvation.[27] There is "a time to keep silent" and "a time to speak," says Ecclesiastes (Eccl 3:7). Gregory explains that it's time to be silent when it comes to God's incomprehensible nature, but time to speak when it comes to all that gives us strength in Jesus Christ.[28] It's time to speak when it comes to what God does for us and what is as such *within* our reach. When dealing with the history of salvation, it is appropriate to use theological language, but we must refrain from trying to capture the inaccessible nature of God theoretically.

25. Gregory of Nyssa, *Oration on the Deity of the Son and of the Holy Spirit* 557.

26. Gregory of Nyssa, *On Not Three Gods* 3.1.42–43.

27. Gregory of Nyssa, *Against Eunomius* 2.1.152.

28. Gregory of Nyssa, *Homilies on Ecclesiastes* 415.17—416.

As described above, Basil had already emphasized how we speak of the general when we speak of the being or nature of something, but of the particular when we speak of the characteristics that belong to the individual. Gregory adds that this should not only be understood as a matter of language. The being of God is the general, indefinite nature of God, which cannot be conceptualized, but is realized in the divine persons. However, the universal and the individual are both something concrete. The common being is not something abstract, purely conceptual, but the collective reality that characterizes the Father, Son, and Holy Spirit. Otherwise, the Father and the Son would in reality be two gods. "God," then, is more than just a common concept that can be attached to the Father and the Son.[29] The concept of God refers in the first place to the Father, whose being is also that of the Son by virtue of the Son's eternal birth from the Father. As the Nicene Creed states, it is the Father who is the one God, but the Father is the source and origin of the Son, who is, then, also God.

Listening to God

Gregory of Nazianzus (c. 329–390) traveled to Constantinople when Emperor Valens died in 378 and was replaced by Theodosius, who was more friendly to Nicene theology. Gregory was also present at the Council of Constantinople in 381, which he presided over for a time. Before he was appointed Bishop of Constantinople, he stayed in a private residence with a small chapel attached. Here he delivered a series of sermons that are now known as the *Five Theological Orations*. There was widespread opposition to Nicene theology in the city of Constantinople, so Gregory had to make a case for the Nicene belief that the Son has the same being as the Father. The sense of the limitations of rational language that prevailed in Basil and Gregory of Nyssa comes to the fore once again.

29. Harnack believed that the nature of God in Cappadocian theology was understood generically and that it reintroduced subordinationism, when the Father was perceived as the origin of the rest of the Trinity. However, this is a simplistic reading. See Zachhuber, *Rise of Christian Theology*, 46–66.

Theology cannot be based on abstract, rational definitions of God, so before we engage in theology, we must listen quietly if we want to learn something about God.[30]

In Gregory's theological orations, it again becomes clear that the limitations of theology have to do with the nature of God. God is essentially hidden from us, like the Ark of the Covenant, which was hidden behind the curtain according to Exodus (Exod 26:31–33). Even the most exalted, heavenly things are far more distant from God than they are from us.[31] Like theologians before him, Gregory understood the story of Moses's encounter with God on Mount Sinai as an expression of God's hiddenness. Moses was not allowed to see God's face, but had to stand in a cleft in the rock so that he could only see God from behind as he passed by. The rock, says Gregory, is an image of God's Word incarnate for us, i.e., Christ. Only when we stand firmly in God's Word can we know anything about God. Language can point to God, but it doesn't help us comprehend God's hidden being.[32]

The trinitarian doctrine of God is not a rational theory of God. The divine "unity in diversity" is rather, Gregory explains, a "paradox" that like a lamp illuminates our thinking about God.[33] Gregory also rejects any tendency towards subordinationism, where the Trinity is understood hierarchically: we value "monarchy," Gregory famously explains, but not understood as the monarchy of a single person.[34] The monarchy that characterizes the Trinity implies a "natural equality," a "harmony of will," and an "identity of action" between Father, Son and Spirit, that point back to their unity. Although there may be a numerical difference between the persons of God, they are equal, since there is no separation in their being. Gregory can also speak of God as "one nature in three individuals," and it can now sound as if it is the Trinity as

30. Gregory of Nazianzus, *Oration* 27.3.

31. Gregory of Nazianzus, *Oration* 28.3.

32. Gregory of Nazianzus, *Oration* 28.6.

33. Gregory of Nazianzus, *Oration* 28.1.

34. Gregory of Nazianzus, *Oration* 29.2.

such that is described as God.[35] In a sermon Gregory makes it clear that "when I say God, I mean the Father, the Son and the Holy Spirit."[36] God is not an isolated person, but, it may seem, rather a community of three persons. The three are one whole in a divinity that consists of three individuals.[37]

Still, this should not be taken to mean that God is simply the Trinity, since in Cappadocian theology it is the Father who is the one God who causes the rest of the Trinity. The Father may to this degree even be called "greater" than the Son, as the Arians argued, insofar as the Father is the cause and origin of the Son. However, as the cause of the Son, the Father is also the source of the Son's equality with the Father, says Gregory.[38] The Father passes on his simplicity and oneness to the Son, so to speak, who is, then, one with the Father.[39] Even if the Father can be described as "monarch," the unity of God precludes any kind of subordinationism that wants to understand the Son as unequal to the Father.

Again, it is crucial that God's being cannot be captured by words. When we speak of God as Father or Son, it only has to do with what the divine persons are in their relations. Words like *father* and *son* do not define the nature of God, but only say something about the close relationship that exists between the Father and the Son.[40] We use the words *father* and *son* for God for lack of better terms. Gregory, similar to Athanasius, argues that we cannot transfer natural human relations to God and conclude that God is

35. Gregory of Nazianzus, *Oration* 33.16. It is debatable to what extent Gregory differs in his view of the "monarchy of the Father" present in the trinitarian doctrine of Basil and Gregory of Nyssa. See Torrance, *Trinitarian Faith*, 321; Beeley, *Gregory of Nazianzus*, 217.

36. Gregory of Nazianzus, *Oration* 38.8.

37. Gregory of Nazianzus, *Oration* 31.9.

38. Gregory of Nazianzus, *Oration* 40.43. Athanasius also admitted that the Father can be called "greater" than the Son, since the Son is begotten of the Father, but states that the latter makes it clear that the Son belongs to the being of the Father, which makes the Son equally God. Athanasius, *Orations Against the Arians* 1.58.

39. Gregory of Nazianzus, *Oration* 42.15.

40. Gregory of Nazianzus, *Oration* 29.16.

"male" just because the words *God* and *father* are grammatically masculine.[41] In Greek, the word *divinity* is feminine, Gregory notes, but, he asks rhetorically, does that mean that God is "female"? The answer, of course, is no, because God is beyond language. When we speak of God as Father and Son, it is to emphasize their common being, not to define it as masculine or anything else for that matter. This is not to say, of course, that Cappadocian theology subscribed to post-modern notions of fluid gender identity, but on the other hand, it would be wrong to dismiss it as hopelessly "patriarchal." Even if we speak of the "monarchy" of the Father, the point is clear enough—we cannot define God's being, but need to speak relationally about the divine persons who are equal because of their common being.

Nothing in creation fits perfectly as an illustration of the triune God. If anything, says Gregory, it would have to be the metaphor of the sun, its rays and its light, which has the same being as the sun.[42] The Trinity can be described as "light and light and light," but the light is one, God is one.[43] "In your light we see light," says a psalm in the Hebrew Scriptures (Ps 36:10), and this can be understood to mean that we receive the light of the Son *from* the light of the Father, *in* the light of the Spirit. However, even that metaphor is insufficient, since ultimately our language is incapable of capturing the reality of God.[44]

The Social Analogy and Its Implications

Trinitarian theology is not only relevant for how we perceive God. It also has an impact on how we view humanity. As created in the image of God (Gen 1:27), humanity reflects God's unity in diversity. This provides the basis for what we sometimes call "the social analogy." The Cappadocians, in their polemic against

41. Gregory of Nazianzus, *Oration* 31.7.
42. Gregory of Nazianzus, *Oration* 31.31–32.
43. Gregory of Nazianzus, *Oration* 31.3.
44. Gregory of Nazianzus, *Oration* 31.33.

Neo-Arianism, regularly noted that different biblical characters may be distinct individuals, but they are, nevertheless, all human.[45] Something similar applies to the divine persons. Although they each have their individual characteristics, they have the same divine being, and for this reason, they are equally God.

The social analogy works back on how we understand humanity. The Trinity can be understood in terms of human relations, but only *if* the latter are understood correctly.[46] According to Athanasius, the Arians were guilty of trying to understand the relationship between the Father and the Son in terms of human relations, when it should really be the other way around.[47] We might say that especially Gregor of Nyssa, in his use of the social analogy, takes note of this and adapts the view of human relations so that they can be used to describe divine relations.[48] Only when humanity is understood as created in the image of the triune God, can human relations be used as an illustration of God.

This is clear in Gregory's letter to Ablabius, where he explains why trinitarian theology does not imply three distinct gods.[49] Gregory argues that although human nature appears in a multiplicity of human persons, it is united in one indivisible unity.[50] In fact, it is almost an abuse of language when we speak of a plurality of humans—at least if we mean a plurality of human *natures*.[51] There is only one, common human nature. When we speak of "persons" in the plural, it implies a separation of individuals, which has to do with each individual's particular characteristics. Similarly, in

45. For example, Gregory of Nyssa, *Letter 38* (traditionally ascribed to Basil). Basil, *Letters* 210.4. Gregory of Nyssa, *On Not Three Gods*.

46. See, however, Behr, *Nicene Faith*, 2:428.

47. Athanasius, *Orations Against the Arians* 1.26.

48. See, however, Behr, *Nicene Faith*, 2:428.

49. Gregory of Nyssa, *On Not Three Gods* 3.1.39–41. However, it is disputed how radically the analogy should be understood. Ayres, *Nicea and its Legacy*, 344–59. See also Behr, *Nicene Faith*, 2:428.

50. Gregory of Nyssa, *On Not Three Gods* 3.1.41.

51. Gregory of Nyssa, *On Not Three Gods* 3.1.39. The point could be made in English, perhaps, that we should not talk of a plurality of human *beings*, but of humanity as one human *being* consisting of a plurality of human *persons*.

God there is only one divine nature, although we can speak of individual divine persons with particular properties. However, unlike humans, who can often disagree, there is unity of will and action when it comes to God. This is emphasized by the fact that we speak of God in the singular.[52] The Trinity is a completely egalitarian community of Father, Son, and Holy Spirit. The Father is the unbegotten cause and origin of the others. God's activities reach us *from* the Father *through* the Son, and are completed *in* the Holy Spirit.[53] There is an order to the Trinity, but this does not mean that the Son and the Holy Spirit are *subordinate* to the Father, or that the three are distinct gods.

While it is only an analogy, this has implications for how we perceive relations between humans. These must also be characterized by equality, because of the unity of human nature. Gregory's outspoken criticism of domination and violence is firmly rooted in his trinitarian theology. The clear distinction between God and creation sets limits to any attempt of humans to rise above each other. It is, says Gregory in his polemics against Eunomius, only because Christ is divine in nature that he has the right to rule over humans.[54] We, on the other hand, are equal because all human persons have the same human nature. Gregory can even argue that revolutions in society occur so frequently because it is practically impossible that humans, who are equal by nature, should not share power. A similar argument underpins Gregory's famous rejection of slavery, as he reasons that the division into master and slave is absurd since it introduces a division of human nature, which is otherwise one.[55] Just as the whole divine being is present in each of the divine persons, so the whole humanity is present in each individual human, who as created in the image of God has infinite value.

In other words, Nicene and Cappadocian theology implies what we might call a *two-tier egalitarianism*. There is a "gap" between the eternal God and creation, but each is characterized

52. Gregory of Nyssa, *On Not Three Gods* 3.1.54–55.

53. Gregory of Nyssa, *On Not Three Gods* 3.1.48.

54. Gregory of Nyssa, *Against Eunomius* 1.1.527–28.

55. Gregory of Nyssa, *Homilies on Ecclesiastes* 336.

by internal equality on its respective level of being.[56] The Nicene Creed does not explicitly exclude all sorts of subordinationism, but as we have seen, it gradually becomes clear that its logic precludes a hierarchical view of the Trinity.[57] This is true even if God the Father is described as the cause and source of the other divine persons, who are not, for this reason, subordinate to the Father. The Cappadocians may have reintroduced an emphasis on the notion of God the Father as "monarch," but they did so *without* compromising the equality of the divine persons. There is a clear distinction between God and humans, but the egalitarian community that characterizes God should be reflected in an equally egalitarian communion between humans.

Such trinitarian theology has an impact on human relations that is still relevant today. In contemporary theology, there are attempts to defend a hierarchical view of humanity based on the supposed subordination of the Son of God to the Father. This is the case, for example, in conservative parts of American and global evangelicalism, where the subordination of women to men is justified by Christ's supposed subordination to the Father.[58] God the Father is the one who commands, while Christ obeys, the argument goes, and this kind of hierarchical structure should be reflected in human relations, it is claimed. Such arguments may seem far-fetched, but they are at least interesting as contemporary examples of how attempts at justifying a particular social order by adjusting trinitarian theology comes into conflict with the classic doctrine of the Trinity.

The subordinationism that to some degree characterized pre-Nicene theology has no place in Nicene and Cappadocian theology. God cannot be divided into ruler and subject.[59] The Father is the origin and cause of the Son, but there is one common will in

56. Cf. Maspero, *Cappadocian Reshaping of Metaphysics,* 57.

57. See, however, Edwards, "Is Subordinationism a Heresy?," 74.

58. According to so-called Eternal Functional Subordination, the Son and the Father may be *ontologically* equal, but the Son is *functionally* subordinate to the Father.

59. Gregory of Nazianzus, *Oration* 42.6.

God.[60] It is only in his human nature that Christ submits to and obeys God. In his divine being, Christ is equal to God—and that is why it is so miraculous that he nevertheless becomes human for our sake. When Christ is said to have taken "the very nature of a servant" (Phil 2:6–8), Nicene and Cappadocian theologians argued that this had to do with his task as incarnate in the history of salvation—not that he is inherently subordinate to God. We have already discussed what this meant for Athanasius in particular. In the following, we will take a closer look at how this works out in the relationship between the doctrine of the Trinity and salvation in Nicene and Cappadocian theology.

60. Gregory of Nazianzus, *Oration* 30.12. See Butner, "Eternal Functional Subordination and the Problem of the Divine Will," 138–39.

5

"For Our Salvation"

Soteriology

THE NICENE CLAIM THAT the Son of God really has the same being as his Father is no mere theoretical subtlety. For theologians who defended Nicene theology, it was at the heart of the gospel that God had become human for our sake. The Christian God is not merely distant, but participates in our condition in order to have fellowship with us. This is arguably the point when the Nicene Creed speaks of the Son of God, "who for us humans and for our salvation descended and became flesh." The discussion about Jesus's identity as God was not just a matter of philosophical definitions. The belief that the Son of God is begotten "of the Father's being" and has the "same being" as his Father plays a crucial role in understanding what it means that God became human to save humans.

Sometimes so-called Arianism is broadly associated with the view that God, being eternal, is incapable of suffering and that it must for this reason be a created, secondary "God" who becomes human in Jesus. We need a God who can suffer—to paraphrase a phrase from Dietrich Bonhoeffer—someone who can actually take part in our mortal conditions.[1] In late antiquity, God was in

1. The German Lutheran pastor and theologian Dietrich Bonhoeffer (1906–1945) is known for the expression that "only the suffering God can

general believed to be unchangeable and incapable of suffering. For Arian theologians, this seems to have been a reason why the Son of God, who suffers for us, must be subordinate and different from God the Father. This view was held, among others, by the Gothic bishop and missionary Ulfilas (c. 311–383). The result was that Gothic theology became Arian rather than Nicene for a long period.[2] That the Son of God has the "same being" as his Father, as stated by the Nicene creed, was a downright "perverse" view, according to Ulfilas. The eternal God is unchanging and impassible, and so it must be a secondary "God," who is capable of suffering, who has become human in Jesus.

For Nicene and Cappadocian theology, this wasn't much of a gospel. If the Son of God is a creature like others, creation will have to be saved by itself, which is hardly good news. Christianity, by contrast, is about God becoming human in order to save humans. This was the core of the gospel for theologians who defended the Nicene Creed. The precise wording that the Son has the "same being" as the Father was less important to begin with. It only became important as it came to be associated with the soteriology (the doctrine of salvation) that was at the heart of Nicene theology. From the perspective of the story of salvation, the Son of God is not primarily a cosmic link between God and creation, but the crucified and risen Christ who restores our broken communion with God. In short, God became human so that humans can become God, as theologians argued. This is the essence of what is often called the "classical" doctrine of the atonement. In the following, we'll have a closer look at what this means in more detail and how it relates to the discussions above on trinitarian theology.

"God Became Human . . ."

There are indications that Arius's theology was not only about the being or nature of God. It may also have impacted how salvation

help." The suffering of God became a theme in twentieth-century theology, as the classical idea of God's "impassibility" was often rejected.

2. See Hanson, *Search for the Christian Doctrine of God*, 104–6.

was perceived. Some scholars have suggested that it was a form of theological *voluntarism* that characterized Arianism.[3] The will of God is the fundamental principle of such theology. The father-son relationship, which according to Nicene theology was eternally in God, was according to Arius the result of a decision. God only became Father as he made the Son by an act of will. The relationship between God the Father and God the Son is not, to this degree, a matter of a natural and mutual relationship. Rather, it consists in unequal and external relations of commanding and obeying. If the Son can be said to participate in the Father, it can only mean that the Son's will conforms with that of the Father.[4] If the Son had the same being as the Father, as in Nicene theology, he would also have had the same will. In that case, there would not be two wills where one commands and one obeys. In Arian theology, however, the Father and the Son do not have a common being, but they do have a moral union.[5]

In other words, Arian theology may be said to understand the relationship between the Father and the Son in terms of *covenant* rather than *being*. Something similar must, by implication, be the case in the relations between God and humans. Although it is difficult to assess from the sources what Arius and his peers actually believed about salvation, it has been argued that the Arian view of salvation must also be understood morally and in terms of a covenantal theology. In this perspective, Christ achieved his status with God through a moral progress that set an example for others.[6] If participation is understood morally—as a community of wills—it is by submitting to and obeying God that humans can have fellowship with God. Christ, in the Arian logic, is not God himself who became human to give humans a share in God, but rather an example to follow.

3. Groh and Gregg, *Early Arianism*, 96. This is slightly anachronistic, since "voluntarism" usually refers to a theological tradition that only became prevalent in the late Middle Ages. See also Torrance, *Trinitarian Faith*, 277.

4. This understanding of participation is (perhaps) Stoic rather than Platonic. Groh and Gregg, *Early Arianism*, 111.

5. See Hilary, *On the Trinity* 8.5.

6. According to Groh and Gregg, *Early Arianism*, 117.

Whether or not this is an accurate representation of Arian soteriology, we can at least say that for theologians like Athanasius, it was not enough. Creation cannot save itself, he noted.[7] This is why it is so important that the Word of God, who became incarnate in Christ, is not just a subordinate, created "God," but truly God, who has become human in order to save humans. God has taken part in humanity's condition so that we can have fellowship with God. That this was Athanasius's view even before writing his works against the Arians, suggests that his understanding of salvation may have at least in part determined his views on trinitarian theology rather than the other way around. Whether Athanasius's important work *On the Incarnation* was actually written as early as *before* the Council of Nicaea in 325 is a matter of debate—if so, he must have been quite young when he wrote it. The book does not discuss the Nicene formulations, but this may also be because it was written after Nicaea, but before new controversies arose from the 340s onward.[8] In any case, what is interesting is that the understanding of salvation expressed in the works against the Arians already exists to some degree before Athanasius sets out to defend Nicene theology in the 340s.

For Athanasius, salvation means first and foremost salvation from death. There are plenty of mythological notions of salvation and perdition in the theology of the early church, but there is an existential clarity when Athanasius speaks of salvation as a matter of life and death. Corruption and death are the natural consequences of sin, but God partakes of humanity's death so that we can again partake in the life that comes from God. Once again, the work of Christ *for us* is at the center. Out of love for humans, the Word of God, the divine *logos*, has stepped into our place.[9] The purpose is to make it possible for humans to participate in God, which, as we have already seen above, is what makes it so important that Christ is truly God.

7. Or more precisely: "no creature can ever be saved by a creature." Athanasius, *Letter to Adelphius* 8.

8. The specific formulations of the Nicene Creed are virtually absent from theology in the years up to the 350s. See Kelly, *Early Christian Creeds*, 254–55.

9. Athanasius, *On the Incarnation* 8.1.

Athanasius unfolds the story of salvation with more or less dramatic depictions of what happened when the Word became human in Jesus Christ. It is, he explains, like a mighty king who settles in a house in a city so that no robbers dare attack the city.[10] Something similar applies when the king of all takes up residence in a human body. Immediately, the enemy's plans against humanity come to an end and the "corruption of death" must give up. From this perspective, death is a collective enemy that threatens to destroy humanity as such. The Son of God had to become human, Athanasius explains, because the human race would have been wiped out if the Savior and Lord of all had not come to put an end to death.

However, "death was absolutely necessary," writes Athanasius, and so the Son of God had to take up residence among us in order to take death upon himself. Jesus gave his body as a "temple to death" to relieve all from responsibility for the "original transgression."[11] Paul could write that "one died for all, and therefore all died" (2 Cor 5:14), and Athanasius affirms that our death is in a sense executed in Jesus's death on the cross. The death of all was completed in the Lord's body, while death and corruption were destroyed by the Word in it.[12] But why did Jesus have to die on a cross? Athanasius responds remarkably that it is only by dying on a cross that one dies with open arms.[13] The point is that Jesus on the cross draws everyone to himself (John 12:32). In doing so, he unites humanity with God, and that is what salvation is all about—communion with God in Christ.

The collectivist way of thinking is echoed in Athanasius's polemic against the Arians. The Son of God came into the world to ransom *all* so that the world could be saved through him. As guilty,

10. Athanasius, *On the Incarnation* 9.3–4.

11. Athanasius, *On the Incarnation* 20.2. It is debatable whether this is a kind of "original sin," as in Augustine, or rather what is sometimes called "original death." In any case, humanity is *collectively* subject to the condition of death because of sin.

12. Athanasius, *On the Incarnation* 20.5.

13. Athanasius, *On the Incarnation* 25.3.

the world was under the "judgment of the law," but the Word of God took judgment upon himself by suffering in the body for all.[14] The Word of God, says Athanasius, has taken on a human body to pay our debt and to give us the "immortality and way to paradise" that we lacked.[15] The Word of God took on human flesh from his mother Mary, the "mother of God." He bore humanity's flesh as his own, and because he was *in* the flesh, its sufferings are his.[16] Athanasius repeats these points in terms of participation when writing on the Nicene Creed. Since humans are incapable of existing on their own, we must participate in the Word of God in order to exist at all.[17] God's Word became flesh to give his body for all so that we can have fellowship with God.[18] We do not just have Christ "outside" us as a teacher, Athanasius stipulates, but "within" us.[19]

Salvation is, in other words, not just *moral* or *covenantal*, but *ontological*.[20] While such notions of salvation is typically associated with Athanasius and "Greek theology," in the Latin west Hilary developed a similar view in his polemics against Arianism. As he puts it, we are in Christ because of the union of the flesh assumed by the Word, and as such humanity is reconciled in "the body of his flesh."[21] In a way, the gospel is not so much about the *possibility* of salvation, but about a salvation that is in principle *already* realized. Faith is necessary to continue to participate in this salvation, but the union between humanity and God is not to begin with the product of individual faith, since it has already occurred in the incarnation of the Word in Christ.

14. Athanasius, *Orations Against the Arians* 1.60.

15. Athanasius, *Orations Against the Arians* 2.66.

16. Athanasius, *Orations Against the Arians* 3.31–32.

17. Athanasius, *On the Council of Nicaea* 11.

18. Athanasius, *On the Council of Nicaea* 14.

19. Athanasius, *Orations Against the Arians* 3.56.

20. This is why the "classic" theory of atonement is also at times called the "ontological" theory of atonement.

21. Hilary, *Commentary on the Psalms* 91.9. See Scully, *Physicalist Soteriology in Hilary of Poitier*, 96.

The doctrine of the Trinity, in other words, conceptualizes the mechanics of the gospel. The precise formulation that the Son of God has the "same being" as his Father only gradually becomes an expression of this specific soteriology. What is crucial is that God became human in order to save humans. The Son of God, who has become human for us, must be divine like his Father if he is to give us fellowship with God. This, we can conclude, is the point when we say that the Son is "God of God," "light of light," and so on, according to the Nicene Creed.

Christ in the Belly of Death

Several of the themes found in Athanasius are repeated in Cappadocian theology. Gregory of Nyssa's *Catechetical Discourse*, a kind of baptismal training, resembles Athanasius's book *On the Incarnation* in many ways. The theoretical efforts in the fight against Neo-Arianism are brought to life in the catechism, which is notable for its dramatic descriptions of salvation. The doctrine of the Trinity and the divinity of Christ is at the forefront. The triune God is the one who speaks, the Word that is spoken, and the Spirit with which God speaks—and once again it is necessary for salvation that it is truly God who becomes human to save us from the power of death. The Word of God is "life itself,"[22] in which all living things participate, but the Word is also the savior who redeems humanity from the captivity of death.

Gregory, like Athanasius, can speak of how God's power, wisdom, goodness and justice must come together in the history of salvation.[23] It is God's wisdom that makes the good intentions to save humans go together with the justice that also characterizes God. Good intentions are useless, Gregory notes, if they stand alone or are "naked." As we've seen, for Gregory, it was not possible to understand God in the abstract. God's power, justice, goodness and wisdom are only experienced concretely. It is in the history of

22. "Life itself" is not an inherent life force, as in modern vitalist philosophies, but the Word of God. Gregory of Nyssa, *Catechetical Discourse* 1.5.

23. Gregory of Nyssa, *Catechetical Discourse* 20.1–5.

salvation that we get to know what Gregory calls God's "philanthropy," i.e., love for humanity.

This is the framework when Gregory goes on to explain how humanity has become the prisoner of death because of sin. As when humans sell themselves into slavery, humanity has surrendered itself to the power of death. Since death, for this reason, has a legitimate claim on humanity, God must ransom humanity by giving something in exchange.[24] The Word of God becomes human in order to liberate humanity. However, this can only be done with an element of deceit—and here the story takes on a rather mythological form, as Gregory compares death to a fish that has swallowed humanity: It is, says Gregory, as when fishing for greedy fish. The divine "hook," the divinity of Christ, must allow itself to be swallowed along with the bait—Jesus's human body. God hides in human flesh so that death will take the bait. However, death is overcome when "life itself" in this way comes to reside in death. Darkness cannot stand where there is light, and death cannot exist where there is life.[25]

It is understandable why the early church's "classical" doctrine of the atonement is often described as *dramatic*.[26] Gregory's depictions are, of course, a mythological representation of something more fundamental. The mechanics are not completely clear "in theory," but there are some obvious principles underlying the narrative. With his death and resurrection, Jesus bridges the gap between death and life.[27] What Gregory describes as "the mystery of God's plan of salvation concerning death and the resurrection from the dead" is that life extends to all of human nature sharing in life as a result of Jesus's resurrection. Jesus does not die and rise for his own sake, but to set humanity free from the power of death.

24. The so-called *ransom doctrine* of the atonement has its roots in Origen, who could also speak of Jesus as an "atoning sacrifice" or "mercy seat," cf. Rom 3:25. Origen, *Commentary on Matthew* 16.8; Origen, *Commentary on Romans* 3.8.2.

25. Gregory of Nyssa, *Catechetical Discourse* 24.4.

26. Aulén, *Christus Victor*, 4.

27. Gregory of Nyssa, *Catechetical Discourse* 16.9.

Although there seems to be a struggle between life and death as if they were two independent and equal powers, this is only so from a superficial point of view. In reality, death is only the absence of life, just as darkness is only the absence of light.[28] God becomes human to illuminate the darkness. Whether Gregory in this context had it in mind that the Son of God is "light of light," as stated in the Nicene Creed, is not clear, but the dramatic descriptions reveal a fundamentally Nicene theology in which Jesus's divinity is crucial to the salvation of humans. The darkness that is death is nothing—it is the absence of being, life and light. Death is not an equal opponent for God, but disappears like dew before the sun when God goes all the way to participate in the human condition.

A God Incarnate and Put to Death

Basil of Caesarea also emphasized how God has come to us in Christ, who is fully divine. And just as important is it that Christ came "in the flesh," as a real human being and not just as a look-a-like, as some believed: "If Christ had not come in the flesh," Basil wrote in a letter, "he could not have restored and reunited with God the humanity that had fallen and been alienated in Adam."[29] The Word of God did not pass through Mary untouched like "water through a pipe," a view that Irenaeus had already criticized, but which was now associated with the theologian Apollinaris of Laodicaea (c. 310–390). The idea was that Christ had brought his own sinless flesh from heaven, but in that case, Basil pointed out, God is not really united with humanity.[30] Only by uniting completely with humanity in the flesh can God save and restore humans.

It is, as we have seen, a common theme in Nicene and Cappadocian theology that God saves by uniting with humanity in

28. Myers, "Patristic Atonement Model."

29. Basil, *Letters* 261.2.

30. The idea, which may have been wrongly ascribed to Apollinaris, reappeared during the Reformation in Menno Simons (1496–1561) and other radical reformers, who believed that Christ brought his own "flesh" from heaven.

Christ.[31] This is not to say that theologians who defended Nicene theology for that reason agreed on every detail of salvation. Gregory of Nazianzus, in an Easter sermon, unlike Gregory of Nyssa, rejected the idea that Jesus was a kind of ransom paid to death.[32] Nor does Jesus die as a payment to God the Father, since God requires no sacrifice for his own sake. The Son of God gives himself, sacrifices himself, for our sake, but not to pay anyone a ransom. Jesus is a "ransom" only in the minimalist sense that with his sacrifice he sets humans free. The principle underlying the story of salvation is that humanity is sanctified by what Gregory calls "the humanity of God." This brings us back to the crucial fact that God has really become *human* in Jesus. It is the "humanity of God" in Jesus that saves. As with Athanasius and Hilary, the idea of our death and resurrection *with* Christ is again central: "We needed an incarnate God, a God put to death, that we might live," Gregory remarkably notes, adding, "We were put to death with him so that we might be clean, and we rose with him because we were slain with him."[33]

The attentive reader may have noticed that the Nicene Creed does not mention that Jesus died, only that he suffered and rose.[34] Gregory of Nazianzus is a good example that this was not necessarily due to a desire to avoid the notion that God experiences death on the cross. Gregory emphasizes that it is, in a sense, really God who suffers and dies on the cross—even though God is immortal and incapable of suffering. It was, as explained above, a common principle in Nicene theology that since Jesus is both God and human, we can attribute all that is unworthy to his human nature, while all that is exalted and miraculous should be attributed to his divine nature. However, according to Gregory, the divine and human natures are so intimately related in Jesus that God, who

31. While this was not a necessary corollary of Nicene theology, the idea is prevalent throughout the fourth century. See Scully, *Human Salvation in Early Christianity*, 1–33.

32. Gregory of Nazianzus, *Oration* 45.22.

33. Gregory of Nazianzus, *Oration* 45.28.

34. In distinction to, e.g., the Apostolic Creed. That Christ was crucified and died is mentioned for the first time in an eastern creed in the Fourth Creed of Antioch from 341. See Kinzig, *History of Early Christian Creeds*, 381.

can neither suffer nor die, nevertheless shares in our suffering and death when Jesus experiences death on the cross.

When Jesus cries out the famous words of the cross, "My God, my God, why have you forsaken me?" (Mark 15:34), it is all of God-forsaken humanity that speaks in Jesus. On the cross, God himself experiences the abandonment of humanity: "We had once been forsaken and rejected," writes Gregory, but "we were then accepted and saved by the suffering of him who could not suffer."[35] Once again, the point is that God shares in our condition so that we can have fellowship with God. The belief that God partakes in our condition is crucial. We should, however, be careful about understanding this in terms of "substitution," if by that we mean that God becomes human so that we can completely avoid suffering and death.[36] God shares in our suffering and death so that we can have fellowship with God *in* suffering and death. In Jesus, the Word of God has united with all condemned humanity to become "all for all," writes Gregory.[37] This is indeed "a suffering God" who has come to our rescue, to paraphrase Bonhoeffer again. Whereas Arianism rationally solved the problem of the suffering God by claiming that it is a secondary, created God who suffers in Christ, for Gregory the incarnation and the atonement are a paradox, as is the doctrine of the Trinity itself.[38]

Gregory, in a sermon, explains how the Word of God, who is "light of light," the source of life and immortality, and so on, "empties himself of his glory for a while, so that I may share in his fullness."[39] The idea comes from the Epistle to the Philippians, where Jesus is said to have emptied himself (or "made himself nothing") by taking the form of a servant (Phil 2:7). That Jesus

35. Gregory of Nazianzus, *Oration* 30.5.

36. As in the later doctrine of Christ's death as "penal Substitutionary atonement." Christ does die in our place, but because of our union with Christ, we also, in a sense, die *with* him.

37. Gregory of Nazianzus, *Oration* 30.21.

38. Myers, "Patristic Atonement Model," 76. This, however, is why the atonement can arguably not really be fitted into a "model."

39. Gregory of Nazianzus, *Oration* 38.13.

humbled himself in his incarnation and death is not, however, to be understood as God being diminished, becoming less divine or even changed by becoming human and subject to suffering.[40] That the Word of God partakes in the human condition in order to restore humans is "a more godlike action" than the act of creation, but God does not become less by humbling himself. On the contrary, "humiliation is the best road to exaltation," as Gregory puts it.[41] Or, to put it even more succinctly, it is exactly by his humiliation that Christ is exalted.

As Gregory of Nyssa also made it clear, it is God's ability to save through powerlessness that shows his power.[42] In other words, Nicene and Cappadocian theology typically maintained the paradox of the incarnation, as it is precisely the *impassible* God who remains impassible, but nevertheless suffers for us in Christ. Gregory of Nazianzus can even talk of the incarnation as a "paradoxical mixture."[43] Although it is "only" as a human that Christ is humbled and dies, in him God nevertheless shares in our suffering. The purpose is not to change anything in God, but, as Gregory puts it, Christ assumes "the poverty of my flesh," that "I may assume the richness of his divinity."

". . . So that We Might Become God"

Just as we have died with Christ, we have also risen with him. This is the gospel message in the Easter sermon preached by Gregory of Nazianzus shortly after his inauguration in 362. Sin and death are put behind us with Good Friday, so that the resurrection can be the truth about us today: "Yesterday I was crucified with Christ, today I am exalted with him," says Gregory, adding that "Yesterday I died with him, today I am raised."[44] Our death and resurrection

40. This is not the same, then, as the "kenotic" theology popular in parts of Protestant theology since the nineteenth century.

41. Gregory of Nazianzus, *Oration* 38.14.

42. Gregory of Nyssa, *Catechetical Discourse* 24.1–4.

43. Gregory of Nazianzus, *Oration* 38.13.

44. Gregory of Nazianzus, *Oration* 1.4–5.

with Jesus breaks with familiar concepts of time when actualized in the life and liturgy of the church. This implies a responsibility for us here and now, since we must live in accordance with the new life we have been given. Paul could talk about humans having become new creatures in Christ (2 Cor 5:17). In his Easter sermon, Gregory picks up the cue and goes so far as to urge his listeners to "become gods" for Christ's sake, "since he became human for our sake." Thus, the story of salvation culminates in the deification of those who participate in Christ.

While this theme is particularly associated with Nicene and Cappadocian theology, there was nothing new to the idea of humans "becoming God." The notion has roots in the theology of Irenaeus and Clement of Alexandria. Irenaeus could speak of the church as those who have been adopted as children of God. They are the ones mentioned when a psalm says that "God appears in the assembly of the gods, among the gods he passes judgment" (Ps 82:1).[45] This does not mean that Christians become little gods in their own right, but that by the "grace of adoption" they are allowed to call God *father*. For Clement, the fact that humans are created *in* the image of God, but also according *to* God's likeness (Gen 1:26), meant that it was humanity's task to grow up to resemble God.[46] The Word of God became human so that we can learn how to become God. In similar terms, Athanasius in his book *On the Incarnation* could speak of the deification of humanity when he concluded that the Word became human in order that we might become God.[47]

Nicene and Cappadocian theology may, perhaps, even be said to be the logical conclusion to more traditional notions of salvation as deification. It is, in other words, a largely *soteriological* point that the Son has the "same being" as the Father. Theologians like Clement and Origen had described salvation mostly

45. Irenaeus, *Against Heresies* 3.6.1.

46. Clement, *Stromateis* 2.19.97.

47. Athanasius, *On the Incarnation* 54.3. These words are often paraphrased with the more concise formulation that "God became man so that man might become God."

in pedagogical and moral terms. Christ was the great teacher and instructor. However, if salvation is participation in God, it must really be God, and not just an intermediary, who has come to have communion with humans in the incarnate Christ. This makes it necessary that Christ has the same being as his Father. The Son of God was not a human who became God, writes Athanasius in his polemic against the Arians, but the Son of God was God who became human in order to deify humans.[48] Humanity can only share in God if God has first taken part in our bodily reality.[49]

This line of thought is expressed perhaps most pointedly by Gregory of Nazianzus with the term *theosis* or "deification," if translated straightforwardly. The idea of salvation as deification may sound far-fetched to a Protestant skepticism towards an overly aspirational spirituality, but its "realist" underpinnings should be kept in mind. The prerequisite for the deification of humans is that Jesus *as* a human is *already* deified for our sake by virtue of the incarnation.[50] Jesus is Christ because of his divinity, which anoints his humanity by his presence.[51] It is not something we have to accomplish ourselves, but something we can participate in by having fellowship with God in Christ. Just as important, salvation as deification is not about rising above one's fellow humans by participating in God's exalted being or nature. When Gregory called for his listeners to "become gods" for Christ's sake, he added very significantly that we become gods when we become all that Christ *became* for us.[52] In this way, deification is a matter of participating in what Christ became in the incarnation. It is, in other words, not about rising above others, but about following the incarnate and humble Christ.

Gregory of Nyssa makes a similar point in a sermon on the Beatitudes. It is only possible to have fellowship with God, he says, by imitating the humility shown by the Word of God in becoming

48. Athanasius, *Orations Against the Arians* 1.39.

49. Athanasius, *Orations Against the Arians* 3.33.

50. Torrance, *Trinitarian Faith*, 139.

51. Gregory of Nazianzus, *Oration* 30.21.

52. Gregory of Nazianzus, *Oration* 1.4–5.

human.[53] It is tempting to give this a modern twist and note with, for example, twentieth-century existential theology that Christianity is not about escaping the human condition, but about being "true to the earth" (Nietzsche)—in light, of course, of the gospel about the God who became human "for us," as the Nicene Creed puts it. In other words, salvation as deification means becoming *truly* human, as Christ did. It is not some abstract ideal, but the *incarnate* Christ who is the image of God that humanity was created to resemble (Gen 1:26). We are, in a sense, called to become what we already are in Christ. The ethical component in Nicene and Cappadocian theology can only come as a conclusion to the story in which God became human for our salvation.

53. Gregory of Nyssa, *Homilies on the Beatitudes* 1.4.

6

"And in the Holy Spirit"

The Nicene-Constantinopolitan Creed

It is reported that 150 bishops attended when Emperor Theodosius convened the Council of Constantinople in AD 381. The purpose was to address a number of theological debates that had been divisive since the Nicene Creed was adopted at Nicaea in AD 325. From the 350s, the view prevailed that the Son might be *similar* to the Father, but that we must refrain from talking about their being or nature.[1] This changed when Emperor Valens was replaced by Theodosius in 379, and Nicene theology came back into favor. As mentioned, Gregory of Nazianzus was for a time at the head of the meeting in 381. Gregory of Nyssa also attended. The rationalistic rejection of any similarity in being between God the Father and the Son, as proposed by Neo-Arianism, had to be addressed, but questions about the status of the Holy Spirit were also up for debate.

1. In other words, a *homoian* theology where the Son is only said to be *similar* to the Father, as opposed to *homoiousian* theology where the Son is *similar in being* to the Father and the *homoousian* theology, like the Nicene theology, which claimed that the Son has the *same being* as the Father. See Kinzig, *History of Early Christian Creeds*, 307–23.

At the Council of Constantinople, the central tenets of the Nicene Creed were reconfirmed and expressed anew with what is now known as the *Nicene-Constantinopolitan Creed*. This creed is, in fact, what we most often refer to when we talk about the Nicene Creed—and probably the closest thing we have to a truly *ecumenical* creed.[2] Interestingly, there is no consensus on exactly how and when the Nicene-Constantinopolitan Creed came into being. It may have been an elaboration of the Nicene Creed, but it is also possible that a local creed was adapted to align with the Nicene Creed. The ambiguity is due to the fact that the creed is not mentioned in the documents from the Council of Constantinople. Strangely enough, the earliest evidence of the Nicene-Constantinopolitan Creed comes from the Council of Chalcedon in 451.[3] It apparently lived a somewhat quiet life until it was brought out of obscurity. However, there are indications that it was actually written in Constantinople in 381, even though it was not given binding status until Chalcedon in 451. Since then, it is widely regarded as the definitive expression of Nicene theology.[4]

To the dismay of Gregory of Nazianzus, there was reluctance at the council in Constantinople to make it absolutely clear that the Holy Spirit is God on a par with the Father and the Son. Gregory withdrew before the meeting reached a conclusion.[5] Nevertheless, the Nicene-Constantinopolitan Creed is notable for its elaboration on the Holy Spirit. This part includes the church and baptism as functions of the Holy Spirit. This makes the Creed a good starting point for discussing the implications of Nicene and Cappadocian theology for how we understand such things as the church and baptism, as will be addressed below.

2. Kelly, *Early Christian Creeds*, 348–57.

3. See, however, Kinzig, "Zwei neuentdeckte Predigten."

4. Unlike the Nicene Creed, the Nicene-Constantinopolitan Creed does not conclude with condemnations of those who speak of multiple *hypostases* in God. This made room for the understanding of God as three *hypostases* with one common being.

5. See his speech to "the 150." Gregory of Nazianzus, *Oration* 42.

The Holy Spirit, Who Is Lord

Given their rejection of the divinity of Christ, it was not surprising that opponents of Nicene theology would also reject the divinity of the Holy Spirit. Those who rejected Nicene theology typically saw the Holy Spirit as subordinate to the Son of God, who was subordinate to God himself. In this way, there was seen to be what could be called a Trinity in three levels. Eusebius of Caesarea, for example, considered the Holy Spirit to be subordinate to the Son, who in turn was subordinate to the Father. However, there were also those who, while acknowledging that the Son of God has the same being as his Father, believed that the Holy Spirit was a created servant of the Father and the Son. This movement would eventually be nicknamed the *pneumatomachians*, the Spirit fighters. They were also known as Macedonians, as they seemed to follow the teachings of a bishop named Macedonius. We might say that their view of the Holy Spirit was due to the fact that the idea of the need for a mediating agent *between* God and humans had not yet been completely abandoned. The Holy Spirit was now ascribed the mediating role that the Son of God had in earlier theology.

The discussion is reflected in the Nicene-Constantinopolitan Creed, where especially the part on the Holy Spirit was laid out in more detail. The original Nicene Creed put the belief in the Holy Spirit in very simple terms: "And in the Holy Spirit." So, there's a belief in the Holy Spirit, but the content of this belief was not laid out in any detail. While we might assume that at least some of what was said about the Son also applied to the Spirit, it was arguably this lack of detail that gave way to the perception that the Holy Spirit was a creature with a being or nature different from God's.

This was the misunderstanding that was at least partially addressed in the final part of the Nicene-Constantinopolitan Creed. While the creed's confession of the Father and the Son largely runs parallel to the Nicene Creed, the final parts beginning with the Spirit stand out:

> And in the Holy Spirit, the lord and giver of life, who proceeds from the Father, who is worshiped and honored with the Father and the Son, who has spoken by the prophets.
>
> And in one, holy, common and apostolic church. We confess one baptism for the remission of sins and expect the resurrection of the dead and the life of the world to come.

Although the creed does not explicitly state that the Holy Spirit has the "same being" as the Father or the Son, it does reveal something crucial about the Holy Spirit's status and function by calling the Holy Spirit "lord" and "giver of life." The Holy Spirit "proceeds from the Father" (John 15:26) and is "worshiped" and "honored" together with the Father and the Son. Clearly, the Holy Spirit plays a central part in the story of the triune God. While it is not explicitly mentioned that the Holy Spirit has the same being as the Father, it would become increasingly clear that the Holy Spirit, like the Son of God, is not just an appendix to faith in God, but is present from the beginning. Since all persons of the Trinity participate in all that God does, the Spirit is also the "creator Spirit," just as the Spirit is at work in all parts of the history of salvation.[6]

The Holy Spirit already played a role in Athanasius's polemic against Arianism, but only gradually did it become clear what the discussion about the relationship between the Father and the Son meant for the divinity of the Spirit. This was largely understood in relation to Christ's work in the history of salvation. In his speeches against the Arians, Athanasius explained that the anointing of Jesus by the Holy Spirit is an anointing of humanity *in him*. This unfolds in an interpretation of the psalm about the king who is anointed by God (Ps 45:7). Jesus is divine and was, for this reason, not anointed for his own sake, but for the sake of humans. The savior is God, says Athanasius, and as such he "supplies" the Holy Spirit himself. Jesus was anointed with the Holy Spirit to provide for the "exaltation and resurrection" of humans and for the "indwelling and

6. The Holy Spirit is not added as a bridge between humans and Christ, but is already present in the incarnation. Zizioulas, *Being as Communion*, 111.

intimacy" of the Holy Spirit.[7] When Jesus received the Holy Spirit, it was we who received it *through* him. Once again, the Holy Spirit is understood in relation to what God does *for us* as a human in the history of salvation. It is the Holy Spirit that adopts humans as the children of God. Without the Spirit, we are strangers to God, but the Holy Spirit connects us to God so that God dwells "in us," while we are "in God" at the same time.[8] The Word became flesh, says Athanasius, so that we can be deified by the Holy Spirit, who through the incarnation has taken up residence in humans.[9]

However, it is still not entirely clear whether the Holy Spirit can be said to have the same being as the Father. Only in Athanasius's letters to Serapion from around 360 does it become clear that the Holy Spirit must be God in this sense. Serapion had noticed that there were some in Egypt who, while recognizing the divinity of the Son, regarded the Spirit as an angel created by God. Among the arguments against describing the Holy Spirit as God was that if the Holy Spirit is "begotten" of God, then the Son of God cannot be "only-begotten," that is, God's only child. On the other hand, if the Holy Spirit is begotten by the Son of God, then the Son must also be Father—but isn't God the Father then the "grandfather" of the Spirit?[10] Athanasius responds that the only appropriate response to such silly questions is silence.[11] As in his speeches against the Arians, he adds that we cannot make human relationships the measure of God. In Scripture, the Son is called the Son of the Father, while the Spirit is called the Spirit of the Father, and this is how we should also speak of the Holy Spirit.[12] Although Athanasius only twice outright writes that the Holy Spirit has the "same being" as the Father, he does make it clear that the whole "triad" of Father, Son and Spirit is one God.[13] Jesus gives us the Spirit (John 14:16),

7. Athanasius, *Orations Against the Arians* 1.46–47.

8. Athanasius, *Orations Against the Arians* 3.24–25.

9. Athanasius, *On the Council of Nicaea* 14; 31.

10. According to Athanasius, *Letters to Serapion* 1.15.1–2.

11. Athanasius, *Letters to Serapion* 3.2.6.

12. Athanasius, *Letters to Serapion* 1.16.7.

13. Athanasius, *Letters to Serapion* 1.17.1.

but it is his *own* Spirit that he gives.[14] The Holy Spirit can only give us communion with God because the Holy Spirit is God himself.

The divinity of the Holy Spirit is elaborated upon in Cappadocian theology. Although Basil of Caesarea was initially reluctant to describe the Holy Spirit straightforwardly as God, he emphasized that it is only through the Holy Spirit that we can come to know God.[15] It is the Holy Spirit who makes us God's children, freeing us to call God *father*. By virtue of the Holy Spirit, writes Basil, we are restored to Paradise and exalted to the kingdom of Heaven.[16] The Holy Spirit blesses us with all the good things we have in store from God. While we wait for the consummation, we behold the reflection of grace by promise and faith as if the consummation was already here. In other words, the Holy Spirit makes it possible to anticipate the kingdom of God. This requires faith, because only by trusting in God can we see what has only been realized piecemeal. It is the Holy Spirit who makes faith possible, as it is only possible to understand the Son if we are first enlightened by the Holy Spirit.[17] This is why the Spirit must be God. The Holy Spirit completes the Trinity in union with the one Father through the one Son, says Basil.[18] As the "Spirit of holiness" (Rom 1:4), the Holy Spirit is equal to the Father and the Son, not subordinate.[19]

The fact that the Holy Spirit is "lord" according to the creed says something about the Holy Spirit not just being an instrument we can use at will. It is the Holy Spirit that gives humans a relationship with God. This is only possible because the Holy Spirit is God on a par with the Father and the Son. This is made clear by Gregory of Nazianzus, who in his theological orations connects the divinity of the Holy Spirit with the deification of the human person: "How," he asks rhetorically, "can the Holy Spirit deify me if the Holy Spirit

14. According to Athanasius, *Letters to Serapion* 1.19.7.

15. Basil, *Of the Holy Spirit* 18.47.

16. Basil, *Of the Holy Spirit* 15.36.

17. Basil, *Of the Holy Spirit* 11.27; 26.64. Cf. Origen, *Commentary on Romans* 4.9.10.

18. Basil, *Of the Holy Spirit* 18.45.

19. Basil, *Of the Holy Spirit* 28.70.

has the same status as me?"[20] The Holy Spirit cannot be a creature, but must have the same being as the Father and the Son. The three are a "single whole," while their different names are due to what is distinct for each person in their mutual relationship.[21] Like the Son, the Holy Spirit is not subordinate to the Father. What can be said about the Father and the Son can also be said about the Holy Spirit—except that the Holy Spirit is "unbegotten" like the Father, or "begotten" like the Son. The Holy Spirit, however, "proceeds from the Father," as the Nicene-Constantinopolitan Creed states. This "procession" of the Spirit is the "mean" between the unbegotten Father and the begotten Son.[22]

Gregory of Nyssa is on to something similar as he clarifies in his letter to Ablabius that while the Son is directly from the Father, the Holy Spirit proceeds *from* the Father, but *through* the Son.[23] The Son does not have a *causal* role in the procession of the Spirit, as does the Father, since the latter is the single cause of the rest of the Trinity. However, the Son may be said to have a *relational* role in the procession of the Spirit.[24] There is a "relational order" between the Son and the Holy Spirit, as we can speak of the Spirit of the Son, but not of the Son of the Spirit.[25] While the Son is only from the Father, the Holy Spirit is from the Father and the Son.[26] This does not mean that the Holy Spirit proceeds from the Son as well, but it is clear that the Son plays a role in the procession of the Holy Spirit.

The latter point is worth noting when considering the so-called *filioque* added to the version of the Nicene-Constantinopolitan Creed typically used in Western churches. From the sixth century, churches in the Latin west added the word meaning "and

20. Gregory of Nazianzus, *Oration* 31.4.

21. Gregory of Nazianzus, *Oration* 31.9–10.

22. Gregory of Nazianzus, *Oration* 31.8.

23. Gregory of Nyssa, *On Not Three Gods* 3.1.55.

24. Behr, *Nicene Faith*, 434. "Surprise: A Greek Filioque?," in Maspero, *Rethinking the Filioque with the Greek Fathers.*

25. Gregory of Nyssa, *Homilies on the Lord's Prayer* 424.3–9.

26. Gregory of Nyssa, *Homilies on the Lord's Prayer* 424.1–2.

the Son" to the creed's descriptions of the Holy Spirit, who thus proceeds "from the Father and the Son."[27] The wording is already found in Latin theologians, such as Hilary and Ambrose (c. 339–397), who noted in his work on the Holy Spirit that the Spirit is not divided by its proceeding from the Father and the Son—and Augustine would later affirm this more systematically.[28] The point was, in many cases, to make it clear against Arianism that the Son is equal to the Father. There are formulations in Athanasius and the Cappadocian theologians that can be understood to imply the *filioque*, but unlike the Western church, the Eastern church has held on to the original formulation in the Nicene-Constantinopolitan Creed.[29] The addition of the *filioque* to the creed has since led to conflicts between the Eastern and Western churches over the exact wording—conflicts that could perhaps have been avoided with the more nuanced formulation where the Holy Spirit proceeds *from* the Father, but *through* the Son, as many Latin authors of the 4th century also put it.

Today, there may be good ecumenical reasons to omit the *filioque*. Saying that the Holy Spirit proceeds "from the Father" does not exclude that the Holy Spirit also proceeds *from* or *through* the Son. However, as the above examples suggest, it is not simply a matter of being for or against the *filioque*. When dealing with the creed, the main issue must be how to assert the equality of *all* three divine persons, including the Spirit, and what this means for how we perceive salvation.

"One, Holy, Common and Apostolic Church"

The Nicene-Constantinopolitan Creed not only adds details to the Holy Spirit but also mentions the church and baptism as it

27. Tertullian described it as the Holy Spirit proceeding *from* the Father, but *through* the Son. Tertullian, *Against Praxeas* 3.

28. Ambrose, *On the Holy Spirit* 1.11.120.

29. Hanson, *Search for the Christian Doctrine of God*, 789. David Bentley Hart has also criticized the notion of a particular "Western" theology based on an implicit *filioque*. Hart, "Myth of Schism."

confesses the belief in "one, holy, common and apostolic church" and the confession of "one baptism for the remission of sins." It is hardly a coincidence that the church is mentioned immediately after the Holy Spirit, as it was believed to establish and give individuals a share in the communion of the church. The church is part of the creed—not because the church is divine in itself, but because the church is the work of the Holy Spirit who is God. When the church is described as "one" and as "common" (or *catholic* in Greek), this emphasizes that the Christian community is not just an association of individual persons or congregations, but a God-given reality. The unity of the church is not the result of human agreements, but comes from the triune God.

The same line of thinking seems to be implied when the church is confessed as "apostolic," although perhaps in a more historical and horizontal sense. That the church is apostolic means that it is based on the tradition of the early church and the apostles. Those who defended Nicene theology argued that their trinitarian theology was rooted in the earliest preaching of the gospel—even if early Christians did not explicitly teach that the Son has the "same being" as the Father.[30] The "heretics," on the contrary, all based their teachings on new ideas, strange to the apostolic preaching. That the church is apostolic means that it—and its teachings—can be traced back to the apostles and Jesus himself. This once again emphasizes the unity of the church by pointing to its historical origins. As a matter of church politics, the belief in "one, holy, common and apostolic church" was needed to ensure uniformity in the church. Such unity was made necessary by the larger political situation, where the unity of the church had to correspond to the unity of the Empire.

Apostolic means "sent out" and could also be translated as "missional." However, we should be careful not to read modern missiological points into it. It quickly became a belief in the early church that the apostles themselves had fulfilled Jesus's command to make disciples of all nations by baptizing and teaching people (Matt 28:19). Jesus's disciples have made disciples of all nations,

30. Athanasius, *Orations Against the Arians* 1.2.

writes Athanasius, and in this way it has been fulfilled what the prophet Isaiah wrote about Jerusalem, that "all your children will be taught by the Lord" (Isa 54:13).[31] This does not mean, of course, that the church does not have a job to do. The church is the bearer of tradition, its task is to pass on what it has received by retelling the gospel in word and action.

Gregory of Nyssa, for example, could speak of the gospel as a narrative of "the manifold wisdom of God" (Eph 3:10) that is now being expressed in the church.[32] Paul, in his letter to the congregation in Rome, had written about how "the invisible things of God" have been clearly seen since the creation of the world (Rom 1:20). Gregory understood this to mean that the history of salvation—everything that has to do with Christ, his incarnation, death and resurrection—has been "visible" since the foundation of the *church*, since the church is that "world" (or order, *cosmos* in Greek) in which God's "manifold wisdom" is expressed. This is, of course, a rather subtle interpretation of Paul's words, but the point is clear enough. The church is a new order, founded by God, with the job of proclaiming the gospel in word and action. This, we may add, is what constitutes the "apostolicity" of the church.

It may be tempting to draw conclusions about contemporary discussions on church order from this. Since the creed expresses the essential features of the church's faith, it could be argued that it also says something about the *theological* foundation on which the church is built. If the church's faith is fundamentally trinitarian, this must also be reflected in its form and order. If the Father, Son, and Holy Spirit constitutes an egalitarian order—a harmony of unity and diversity—then the church, it could be argued, must be understood equally as an egalitarian community if it is to reflect the triune God that it preaches. Of course, this would be in many ways a "modern" view of the church, which does not correspond well to that of the time. As is clear from the canons of Nicaea and other councils, the church was a quite hierarchical institution, with strict rules for participation in its life. These particular structures

31. Athanasius, *Orations Against the Arians* 1.59.

32. Gregory of Nyssa, *Homilies on the Song of Songs* 8.384–85.

do not, however, follow by necessity from either the creed itself or Nicene theology more generally.

In any case, the church is more than just a voluntary association of individuals. The latter could perhaps be argued to follow from an "Arian" covenantal theology, but in Nicene theology the church is a participation in the triune God.[33] This is perhaps the "ecumenical" take-away to be made from the above. The "common" church is a God-given reality prior to the particular form and order it takes in local congregations in specific historical contexts. The fact that Nicene theology was in many ways revolutionary in comparison to previous views, does not mean that the creed is useless as a universal expression of what must be understood as at least *implicit* in the Christian faith. The creed has ecumenical significance because it says something about what *should* be common to all Christian denominations—faith in the triune God.

One Baptism for the Remission of Sins

With the above in mind, it seems fitting that baptism in the Nicene-Constantinopolitan Creed is mentioned only after the church. The church is presupposed in the confession of "one baptism for the remission of sins." It is through baptism—and the catechetical training associated with baptism—that the church passes on the faith to the individual believer. Theologians could speak of baptism as "enlightenment" where the baptized person receives the mystery of faith.[34] In baptism, the Holy Spirit enlightens the baptized, who gains insight into the relationship between the Father and the Son. Baptism is an "anointing" with the Holy Spirit, where the baptized person shares in Christ and in this sense becomes a "Christian," i.e., anointed.

Athanasius, in his polemic against Arianism, explained baptism in clearly trinitarian terms. The whole Trinity works in union when baptism takes place. The Father baptizes the person whom

33. Torrance, *Trinitarian Faith*, 277. See also Hilary, *On the Trinity* 8.5.

34. E.g., Gregory of Nazianzus, *Oration* 40.3. Basil, *Of the Holy Spirit* 15.35.

the Son baptizes, and the person whom the Son baptizes is sanctified by the Holy Spirit.[35] This means that baptism is a work of God. It is God who anoints the person being baptized. This also suggests, it could be argued, that the meaning of baptism is not so much inherent in the ritual itself. When the creed speaks of "one baptism," it may be helpful to distinguish between baptism as a ritual act and the one reality to which baptism refers.[36] It is, as we have seen, not only in baptism that God and humans are united, but baptism derives its meaning from the life, death and resurrection of Jesus, where God has in principle already united with humanity.

The "purification from sins" referred to in Hebrews (Heb 1:3) is not primarily an event in the life of the individual, but, as Athanasius puts it, something that took place in the incarnation of Christ.[37] Similarly, as a ritual, baptism derives its meaning from Jesus's life and his own baptism in the Jordan, which, according to Nicene logic, happened not for his own sake, but for ours. Athanasius explained that since God and humanity are united in Jesus, when he is washed *as* human in the Jordan River, it is we who are washed *in* him and *by* him.[38] When Jesus is anointed with the Holy Spirit as a human, it is we who are anointed *in* him. Athanasius can even say outright that "when he is baptized, it is we who are baptized in him." This is how Jesus provides the Holy Spirit in his work *for us*.[39]

To this degree, it could perhaps even be argued that Jesus's baptism is the "one baptism," from which all other baptisms derive their meaning. In a similar vein, Hilary argues that humanity in Christ was in a sense reborn in his baptism.[40] On the other hand,

35. Athanasius, *Orations Against the Arians* 2.41.

36. Cf. the distinction between baptism as *baptismos* and *baptisma*. Torrance, *Trinitarian Faith*, 293.

37. Athanasius, *Orations Against the Arians* 1.55.

38. Athanasius, *Orations Against the Arians* 1.47–48.

39. Athanasius, *Orations Against the Arians* 1.46–47.

40. Hilary, *Commentary on the Psalms* 2.29. See also Scully, *Physicalist Soteriology in Hilary of Poitiers*, 98–99.

it was commonly believed in the early church that humans are not by nature "children" of God, but only become so by adoption in baptism. For example, Athanasius noted that when we can pray the Lord's Prayer in connection with baptism, it is because in baptism we have come to share in Christ's relationship with God the Father.[41] It is not, however, only in baptism that humanity is united to Christ, but what happens in baptism presupposes what has already happened in what Christ has done for us. In this way, the baptism of the individual believer may be said to be a matter of aligning with what is in principle already real in Christ.[42]

Something like the above seems to be the point in a sermon delivered by Gregory of Nazianzus in connection with a baptismal service. Here, Jesus's baptism in the Jordan forms the background for the upcoming baptism. "Jesus rises from the water," says Gregory, and adds significantly that "The world rises with him." The focal point is Jesus's divinity: "The Spirit comes to him as to an equal, bearing witness to his divinity."[43] This is the narrative that forms the background for the baptism that takes place now. In a way, because of what Gregory called "the humanity of God," we as humans already share in his baptism. This does not mean that we need not baptize now. On the contrary, baptism is an active participation in a reality that in principle already exists, but which we enter into concretely in baptism. As "anointing" and "enlightenment," baptism implies a task for the baptized. In short, Gregory explains, baptism can be understood as a covenant with God for a different life.[44] The person being baptized was clearly expected to live in accordance with Christ's teachings. This covenantal, moral aspect, however, derives its meaning from a deeper ontological reality that is already there because of what Christ has done.

41. Athanasius, *Orations Against the Arians* 1.34.

42. With Paul's logic of reconciliation in mind (2 Cor 5:11–20), we can perhaps say that because Jesus has been baptized for us, we must now be baptized with him.

43. Gregory of Nazianzus, *Oration* 39.16.

44. Gregory of Nazianzus, *Oration* 40.8.

It might seem obvious to us that everyone can and should be baptized. However, in the fourth century, it was still common to baptize only confessing adults.[45] Athanasius justifies this with reference to Jesus's command to make disciples of all nations by baptizing and teaching them (Matt 28:18–20). The Savior *first* commanded to make disciples, Athanasius explains, in order for the proper faith in the Trinity to precede baptism.[46] Gregory of Nyssa, in his catechism, even claimed that baptism is only valid if the baptized person has the right understanding of the triune God whose name they are baptized into. The central teaching of Nicene theology, that the Son has the "same being" as the Father, is again crucial. If we believe, as the Arians do, that Christ is a creature like others, we are baptized into a creature, but not God. Baptism is a "birth from above," says Gregory (John 3:3), but it can only be so if we understand what it means to be baptized into the eternal God rather than a creature.

Gregory of Nazianzus similarly encourages baptizing children only when they understand at least something of the meaning of baptism.[47] However, it should be noted that although these theologians preferred what today is sometimes called "believers' baptism," they did not reject the validity of infant baptism for that reason. In fact, infant baptism would eventually become the norm. Origen had already justified infant baptism on the grounds that humans are born with a sin that must be washed away, something like what we today call original sin.[48] The fact that infant baptism could become commonplace without much controversy was probably also due to the church being seen as the foundation for the individual's faith, rather than the other way around. As argued, the church is not just an association of individual believers, but

45. Tertullian and Justin Martyr, for example, both argued that baptism should be free and conscious. Tertullian, *On Baptism* 18.4; Justin, *First Apology* 61.

46. Athanasius, *Orations Against the Arians* 2.42. A similar argument was made during the Reformation by Erasmus of Rotterdam and the Anabaptists.

47. Gregory of Nazianzus, *Oration* 40.28.

48. Origen, *Commentary on Romans* 5.9.11.

it is rooted in the triune God and passes on its common faith to individuals through baptism and teaching.

Crucially, baptism in Nicene and Cappadocian theology, as described above, derives its meaning from the story of Jesus's baptism *for us*. It is not the personal qualities of the baptized that are the focal point of baptism, but the reality that applies in Christ. As a practice—ordinance or sacrament—baptism proclaims that the story of Jesus is also the personal story of the individual being baptized. To be baptized is to participate in the story told by the gospel in a concrete and tangible way. In baptism, the baptized person receives the reality of baptism as their own, personally. Regardless of how we practice baptism in our churches today, what matters is that each individual baptism derives its meaning from what is in principle already real in Christ.

7

"The Life of the World to Come"

Eschatology

Church history offers a wealth of speculation about the end times, judgment day and the afterlife, heaven and hell. Not much is said, however, about any of this in the creeds mentioned above. The Nicene Creed speaks of Jesus having "ascended into heaven," from where he "comes to judge the living and the dead," but that's about it. The focal point is Jesus and his identity as the Son of God who has the same being as his Father. The Son of God has become human for our salvation, as the creed puts it, but when and how he "comes" and what the judgment consists of seems to be of secondary importance.

The Nicene-Constantinopolitan Creed states in more detail that Jesus will "come again in glory" to "judge the living and the dead." It adds that "there shall be no end to his kingdom," as the angel said to Mary when announcing that she would give birth to Jesus (Luke 1:33). This again emphasizes Jesus's divinity, although perhaps in the creed it is most of all a polemical gesture against alternative views of the kingdom of God. A more proper reference to an actual hope for eternity is only found after the confession of the Holy Spirit. Here it concludes that "we expect the resurrection of the dead and the life of the world to come." This is how the Nicene-Constantinopolitan Creed ends—not with a confession or a belief, but with an expectation.[1]

If one wants to build the rest of theology on eschatology, as sometimes suggested by contemporary theology, there is not much help to be found in the creed. Faith is directed at the triune God and what Jesus has done in the history of salvation. The expectation of something future must follow from what *has* happened. Hope is in God, rather than what we expect from God, but that is precisely why it is not a vague hope or unfounded optimism. So-called *eschatology* deals with the "last things" (the *eschaton* in Greek), but it can only do so in light of the church's confession of the triune God whom we already know through Christ. In the following we will take a closer look at some of the eschatological views that were expressed in Nicene and Cappadocian theology, focusing on how these views developed within the context of trinitarian theology.

The Life of the World to Come

In the early church, there were a range of ideas about how things would all end. To begin with, there was a widespread belief in a literal millennial kingdom where Christ would reign with his chosen ones who would be raised from the dead before the rest of humanity. Something like this was held by Justin Martyr and Irenaeus, among others. Eventually, the rest of humanity would be resurrected for judgment. Tertullian had some rather harsh ideas about the punishment of the wicked in the afterlife, while Alexandrian theology offered more optimistic ideas about the "restoration of all things" (the *apokatastasis pantôn* in Greek) and the salvation of all. Gradually, the millennial kingdom was also perceived more symbolically as a spiritual reality that had already begun with Jesus and the establishment of the church. In this respect, a partial "demythologization" of earlier concepts of salvation and damnation,

1. See Kinzig, *History of Early Christian Creeds*, 374.

judgment, heaven and hell, and so on, was already taking place in the theology of the early church.

For Athanasius, salvation meant primarily salvation from death. Jesus is the "common savior" of all humans, because through him all humans come to share in life again.[2] However, Athanasius could also warn against judgment, "eternal fire" and the "darkness outside," biblical concepts that he does not, however, elaborate on much further.[3] The resurrection means that justice can be served, but what exactly this implies is unclear. In many respects, Athanasius's thinking is similar to Origen's, but whether Athanasius also adopted the belief in the restoration of all things is debatable.[4] The recurring line of thought in the polemic against the Arians is that Christ is God who became human for us, and that the incarnation therefore has significance for all humanity.

The same line of thinking is present in Hilary, who also seems to have seen salvation as in some sense already achieved by the union of God with humanity in Christ. In a way, because of our union with Christ, we have already died and risen with him. This can sometimes sound like an almost "realized" eschatology, where the end has already come. That would probably be too much to put into it, however, since salvation is also something future that does not for this reason happen "automatically." Faith and its fruits are necessary to keep the participation in God achieved by Christ.[5] However, because Christ is God, who in his life, death, and resurrection has taken our place, we can at least say that salvation is *also* real here and now.

When the Nicene-Constantinopolitan Creed speaks of the "world to come," it can also be translated as "the age to come" (or *aeon* in Greek). This is hardly to be understood as a heavenly realm where we can finally escape from creation—that would be Gnosticism—but as the created world freed from corruption and death, in a renewed, restored form. When the creed speaks of the

2. Athanasius, *On the Incarnation* 52.1.

3. Athanasius, *On the Incarnation* 56.

4. See, however, Ramelli, *Christian Doctrine of Apokatastasis*, 241–55.

5. Hilary, *Commentary on the Psalms* 51.16.

resurrection of the dead—rather than the "resurrection of the flesh" as in, for example, the Apostolic Creed—the point is hardly that we must escape from the body to "go to heaven," as is believed in some forms of popular religion. Gregory of Nyssa, for example, emphasized how participating in the unity of God must imply a unity of body and soul.[6] The expectation of the world to come and the resurrection of the dead must, rightly understood, be an expectation that creation will be freed from the power of death and corruption, and thereby transformed. This "expectation" of a universal resurrection and the "regeneration of the universe" (cf. Matt 19:28) is based, says Gregory, on the particular experience of the resurrection of Christ.[7]

Resurrection not only means that the dead are brought back to life, but it involves a transformation that breaks with all our conceptions about how things work. This is the view expressed in a series of sermons from the 380s by John Chrysostom (c. 347–407), then bishop of Antioch. In the sermons, delivered against the so-called Neo-Arians, the incomprehensibility of God, as with the Cappadocians, is made an argument for not separating the Son from the Father. It is this incomprehensibility of God that, so to speak, breaks into the world in the incarnation of Christ. The incomprehensibility of God, however, shows itself most clearly in the resurrection, as it breaks with the power of death and all the limitations that characterize creation.[8] Rational thinking is unable to describe the resurrection, Chrysostom explains, as the resurrection goes far beyond human nature and the way things normally work in the world. When the Lord was resurrected, his body not only returned to the earth, but it "went up to heaven," and caused "the whole world to rise with him." Since the resurrection breaks with everything that can be grasped by rational thinking, it is only faith that makes it possible to know what Paul refers to as "the power of his resurrection" (Phil 3:10). Only by faith, says

6. Gregory of Nyssa, *Homilies on the Beatitudes* 7.5.

7. Gregory of Nyssa, *On the Human Image of God* 221.

8. John Chrysostom, *On the Incomprehensible Nature of God* 2.44–45.

Chrysostom, can we trust that a mortal body could be resurrected to a new and unlimited life.

This is a good reason why we should be careful not to formulate too precise theories of the resurrection and the world to come—again, eschatology is not about making the future comprehensible, but an expectation that derives its meaning from the incarnation, life, death, and resurrection of Christ. The end of all things is hidden from us, Athanasius wrote in his speeches against the Arians, just as the limit of life is hidden from each of us.[9] Jesus tells his disciples that "it is not for you to know times or hours" (Acts 1:7). Jesus knows, but it is not good for humans to think too much about how and when things ends. The limit of each human life is, for this very reason, hidden by the Word, just as the limit of the whole is hidden. "In the end of it all is the limit of each one," says Athanasius, "and in the limit of each one the end of it all is brought together." In this way, the larger perspective connects to the small, but as forming a limit to human comprehension.

Following God's Word

Athanasius explains that when the Word has hidden from us both the end of the world and the limit of the individual, it is so that we may live one day at a time, and "advance day by day as if called."[10] It is precisely our ignorance that allows us to take things as they come one day at a time. God calls to the expectation of the world to come, so to speak, but such expectation, it seems, must be an open attitude of attention rather than an attempt to grasp the future by formulating complicated theories about what the future holds. The expectation of eternal life is not for this reason, however, a passive expectation—quite the opposite. It is precisely because we do not know the end in detail that we are called to act here and now. The life of the Christian is, to paraphrase Christoph Blumhardt,

9. Athanasius, *Orations Against the Arians* 3.49.

10. Athanasius, *Orations Against the Arians* 3.49.

an "active expectation" of the kingdom of God breaking into the world in surprising new ways.[11]

Athanasius quotes Paul, who speaks of reaching out after what lies ahead and forgetting what lies behind (Phil 3:13).[12] Such reaching-out-after—so-called *epektasis* in Greek—had already been discussed by Clement of Alexandria and Origen. For Clement, the future was something that can be anticipated here and now in faith and hope culminating in love. In this way, the expectation of the "life of the world to come" has implications for life in the present. It may be noted that common translations of the Nicene Creed say that Jesus "*will* come to judge the living and the dead," but it can also be translated to simply say that he "*comes* to judge the living and the dead." Perhaps we shouldn't read too much into this, but it does leave room for an interpretation of the creed where Jesus will not only come sometime in the future, but also comes to us in every moment here and now.

At any rate, the notion of the Christian life as a reaching out after God plays an important role in Cappadocian theology, especially Gregory of Nyssa. The order and sequence that characterizes the history of salvation in his *Catechetical Discourse* suggests that salvation is imbued with an openness to the future, which can be described as a constant following of God's Word.[13] When Paul can speak of dying "every day" (1 Cor 15:31), Gregory explains, it is because at every moment he "died to the past and forgot everything that lay behind."[14] This is what the bride experiences in the allegorical reading of the *Song of Songs*. The Spirit continuously heals by striking the soul whose very hopelessness becomes the occasion of hope in Christ.

This notion of reaching-out-after God is also related to the distinction between the infinity of God and the finitude of

11. Christoph Blumhardt (1842–1919) was a German Lutheran pastor and theologian known for his eschatology and focus on the kingdom of God in the present.

12. Athanasius, *Orations Against the Arians* 3.49.

13. Gregory of Nyssa, *Catechetical Discourse* 20.5.

14. Gregory of Nyssa, *Homilies on the Song of Songs* 12.366–67.

creation, which was crucial in the debate on the Trinity. Contrary to common philosophical ideals of the time, it makes no sense to strive for immutability, since human nature as created is inevitably subject to change. Human life is like castles of sand on the beach that disappear in an instant in the waves, says Gregory in a sermon on Ecclesiastes.[15] However, we also experience the mutability of life as a continuous becoming in the good when we experience growth and new life. Only God is eternally "self-identical," but the soul is always being created, and is, as such, always something different to itself.[16] This also applies to the world to come, which is not static, then, but must be characterized by life and movement.

This is what Moses learned when he only got to see God from behind (Exod 33:18–23).[17] The "luminous darkness" that he experienced made him realize that we only know God by following the Word.[18] The Christian life culminates not in a diffuse oneness with God, but in following Christ in practice.[19] There is again a trinitarian aspect to this line of thought. As with Gregory of Nazianzus, the rock in which Moses must stand to see God depicts Christ: "He who finds good finds it in Christ," affirms Gregory of Nyssa.[20] Christ is not just a temporary step on the way to a mystical union with God, but the center of our relation to God.

This is, one might say, the dynamics at work in the defense of Nicene theology.[21] The belief that the Son of God has the same being as his Father is not abstract speculation, but has to do with what it means to have communion with God. Where Athanasius and Gregory of Nazianzus spoke of humans "becoming God," Gregory of Nyssa was more careful, but emphasized instead how we must continually reach out after God. The infinity of God means that we will never be finished with God. If we can speak of deification,

15. Gregory of Nyssa, *Homilies on Ecclesiastes* 289.18.

16. Gregory of Nyssa, *Homilies on the Song of Songs* 6.174.

17. Gregory of Nyssa, *On the Life of Moses* 2.239.

18. Gregory of Nyssa, *On the Life of Moses* 2.243–52.

19. Gregory of Nyssa, *On the Life of Moses* 2.317–19.

20. Gregory of Nyssa, *On the Life of Moses* 2.248.

21. See Ayres, *Nicea and Its Legacy*, 302ff.

it is not an end goal, but a continuous movement in communion with the triune God. That God as infinite cannot be defined only emphasizes, in other words, how the "expectation of the world to come" must consist in a continuous openness to the future rather than a particular set of doctrines about eschatology.

The Restoration of All Things?

Paul's first letter to the church in Corinth had long held a central place in eschatology. Origen regularly emphasized one particular passage that put salvation into a larger, cosmic perspective. Paul famously explained that just as all die with Adam, all will be made alive with Christ (1 Cor 15:22–28). This does not happen all at once. First Christ arises, then those who "belong to Christ," i.e., Christians, we must assume. Christ will be king until all "powers and authorities," including death, are subject to him, and then Christ will hand over the "kingdom" to God the Father. Finally, he will also be made subject to God, so that God can be "all in all" (1 Cor 15:28).

While this neatly encapsulates the history of salvation, it does seem to raise a problem in relation to trinitarian theology. If Christ is to "hand over" or "surrender" the kingdom to God the Father, how does this fit with the Nicene-Constantinopolitan Creed, when it says of Christ that "there shall be no end to his kingdom"? This particular formulation in the creed may be directed at Marcellus of Ancyra (died c. 374), a theologian who was originally allied with Athanasius, but became known for the view that Christ only temporarily establishes his kingdom in the history of salvation. Marcellus was eager in his defense of the Nicene Creed and the view that the Son of God has the same being as his Father. According to his opponents, however, he went too far and, like Sabellius, ended up in a form of modalism where the Son of God only temporarily has an independent existence. This is why his kingdom had to end at some point. Marcellus seems to have abandoned this view eventually, but it continued to have adherents. At the same time, the Arians against Nicene theology made use of the words of

Paul about the Son submitting to the Father. This submission, they argued, suggests that Christ is subordinate to God and therefore does not have the same being. Paul's words had become problematic, to say the least.

Gregory of Nazianzus, in his theological orations, polemicizes against both views that misunderstand Paul, each in their own way. It is true that Christ "submits" to God, but he does not do so on his own behalf. When Christ submits to God, he does so on behalf of humanity, so that humanity can be saved through his submission. It is our lack of submission that he takes upon himself so that we in turn can be submitted to God through him: "As long as I refuse to submit to God," Gregory explains, "so long is my lack of submission attributed to Christ."[22] The kingdom of God is eternal, but Christ temporarily submits to God on behalf of humans. Christ does not cease to be God for that reason. When the restoration comes and God becomes "all in all," it is not only God the Father but also Christ who becomes "all in all."[23]

It may seem natural to conclude, like Origen, that all humans will eventually share in the kingdom of God. This, at least, seems to be how Gregory of Nyssa understood Paul's words that God will become "all in all." Christ will reign until he has put all his enemies under his feet (1 Cor 15:25). Gregory explains that this must be understood in relation to the dynamics of the kingdom of God.[24] The enemy is defeated when all opposition to the good is eliminated. When this has happened, Christ will hand over the kingdom to God the Father. This does not mean that Christ ceases to reign, however, but that everything is brought together with the triune God. Even God's enemies will then receive "a trace of divinity" in them, i.e., immortality, with the result that death also disappears. Submission to God means participation *in* God. Through Christ, we are submitted to God, but, adds Gregory, not in the sense of a kind of "slavish subservience." Rather, by being united with God, we come to share in a "kingship, an incorruptibility and a blessing"

22. Gregory of Nazianzus, *Oration* 30.5.

23. Gregory of Nazianzus, *Oration* 30.6.

24. Gregory of Nyssa, *On the Final Subjection of Christ* 27–28.

that "lives in us." It is because Christ *remains* God while submitting to God the Father on our behalf, that he can bring all things together with God. Ultimately, therefore, no one will be excluded from salvation.[25]

As in the works of Origen, there is in Gregory a notion of a "fire" in the afterlife that will purify those who have not been purified in this life through baptism and a holy life. In Gregory's dialogue *On the Soul and the Resurrection,* his sister Macrina explains that even if salvation happens as by force, it aims at freedom. To be saved is to be brought back to the original freedom we were created with, but which is now hidden by our shame.[26] The goal is for humans to become united to God so that God can ultimately become "all in all." To Macrina, this involves sharing in God's autonomy and self-determination. Participating in God does not mean submitting to an external power, but is a matter of sharing in the freedom and love that belong to the triune God.

As indicated, the notion of the restoration of all things was often linked to the defense of Nicene theology.[27] This does not mean that a notion of the restoration of all things is *the* "orthodox" doctrine of salvation, or that some belief in the salvation of all is implicit in the creed. It merely shows that the theology produced in defense of the doctrine of the divinity of Christ was at times thought along these lines. As mentioned, there were a variety of different views at play in the theology of the early church. It wasn't until the Middle Ages that theology was streamlined so that a double outcome of salvation and damnation became the only tenable option. The classical creeds of the fourth century, on the other hand, allow for breadth in eschatology, which, in the end, need not be more complicated than an expectation of "the life of the world to come."

25. Gregory of Nyssa, *On the Final Subjection of Christ* 21.

26. Gregory of Nyssa, *On the Soul and the Resurrection* 100; 103–4.

27. Ramelli, *Christian Doctrine of Apokatastasis,* 823.

8

The Trinity Re-Imagined

The Legacy of Nicaea

MOST OF THE THEOLOGIANS discussed above wrote in Greek. This is largely due to the fact that many of the debates about trinitarian theology took place in the eastern part of the Roman Empire. However, there were also a number of Latin theologians who defended Nicene theology in the western part of the Roman Empire. We have already had a look at Hilary of Poitiers (c. 310–367), who during his exile in Phrygia formulated a defense of the Nicene Creed and its theology. Around the same time, the Roman Neo-Platonic philosopher Marius Victorinus (c. 290–364), after his conversion to Christianity, was able to use his philosophical skills against the "Arians." There were other theologians in the West, including Ambrose and Jerome, who also drew on Greek theology, but it was Augustine who most significantly contributed to thinking through the legacy of Nicaea in a Latin context.

Augustine of Hippo (c. 354–430) has largely set the standard for both Roman Catholic and Protestant theology. In recent years, however, he has been criticized for creating a theology that deviated from the Eastern church on key points—for example, with the doctrines of original sin and predestination, but also in trinitarian theology. The "Latin," Augustinian view of the Trinity is often described as in opposition to the "Greek" view of the Trinity. Greek theologians began with the divine persons, it is argued, while in Latin theology, God's one being precedes God's persons.[1] The problem with this way of thinking is that the personal and concrete reality of God risks becoming secondary to an abstract, philosophical notion of God.

However, there are reasons to be skeptical of such simplistic oppositions.[2] The binary distinction between "Latin" and "Greek" has often had church-political rather than genuinely theological reasons. While there are certainly differences, we must not lose sight of continuity. Augustine belongs to the story as it is the form he gives to Nicene theology that becomes common in the West. Once again, trinitarian theology is best understood in relation to how we perceive salvation. We'll look at this in more detail below, and conclude with a quick look at how the Nicene and Augustinian legacy was received in Lutheran theology during the Reformation.

On the Trinity

The Latin church in the western part of the Roman Empire largely derived its trinitarian theology from Tertullian. That God is "one being in three persons" is often taken to encapsulate this theology. The theological and philosophical details of Nicene theology first became part of the Latin tradition with Hilary of Poitiers, as described above. For Hilary, it was crucial that God can only be understood through God himself. We as humans have no ability to gain insight into the mysteries of God, but must wait for God to reveal himself through his Son, who in order to reveal God must be God.[3] Neo-Platonic philosophy, which played a role in the

1. See Zizioulas, *Being as Communion*, 88–89.

2. The distinction between a Latin theology based on God's "being" and a Greek theology based on God's "persons" has its roots in the French church historian Theodore de Régnon. Régnon, *Études de Théologie Positive sur la Sainte Trinité*, 251. However, see Hart, "Myth of Schism."

3. Hilary, *On the Trinity* 5.20–21.

discussions about the nature of God in the East, was, however, also brought into play by Marius Victorinus in defense of the doctrine that the Son of God has the "same being" as his Father. These were the theologies that formed the background when Augustine began his reflections on the Trinity, even if he did not adopt their points one by one.

Augustine's doctrine of the Trinity is largely an attempt to defend Nicene theology, as he understood it, against contemporary remnants of "Arianism." Augustine's writings against the so-called Arians indicate that theological views similar to Arius's and later theologians like Ulfilas were not yet extinct at the turn of the fifth century. Augustine, in his dialogue with Maximinus, at a late age polemicized against Gothic Arianism, which he had become acquainted with when the Gothic commander Sigiswulf had come to North Africa. Sigiswulf brought with him the bishop Maximinus, whom Augustine in his dialogue presents as defending a theology that is strongly subordinationist. The Son of God is similar to the Father, but not in his being or nature, the Gothic bishop argued. The unity of the Father and the Son is moral in character, as the Son obeys while the Father commands—which aligns well with the Arian theology described above.[4]

This is a clearly subordinationist view of God that Augustine was up against. The metaphor of light still plays a role in trinitarian thinking, but it was understood hierarchically by Maximinus. Enlightenment, he argues, comes "down by stages" from one author, God the Father. We receive enlightenment through the apostles, who have their light from the Holy Spirit, whose light is from Christ, who in turn has his light from the Father who sent him.[5] The Holy Spirit has received from Christ, who has his teachings from the Father. This, according to Maximinus, also means that the Holy Spirit is subject to Christ, who is subject to the Father.[6] Augustine's view in the dialogue, on the other hand, is that Christ illuminates through the Holy Spirit, but that conversely it is also

4. Maximinus according to Augustine, *Answer to Maximinus* 12.

5. Maximinus according to Augustine, *Answer to Maximinus* 4.

6. Maximinus according to Augustine, *Answer to Maximinus* 10.

the Holy Spirit who illuminates through Christ. The relationship of the divine persons is characterized by reciprocity and for this reason they are equal. Their power is equal, their being is one, and their divinity is the same, says Augustine.[7]

Augustine adopted large parts of Nicene theology, which is probably most evident in his books *On the Trinity*. It is often mentioned that Augustine by his own admission was not particularly good at Greek, but several of the most important Greek theologians had been translated into Latin by his time. It should therefore come as no surprise that Augustine's defense of Nicene trinitarian theology bears similarities to that of Athanasius and the Cappadocians—even if Augustine does rethink the doctrine of the Trinity at some points. Again, the equal relationship between the Father, the Son and the Holy Spirit is crucial. The egalitarian view of God that characterized Nicene and Cappadocian theology is echoed in Augustine.

The first several sections of Augustine's work on the Trinity deal with the Son's equality with the Father. As with Athanasius, this requires reading Scripture with the right perspective. Some verses can be understood to deal with the Son being equal to the Father, while others deal with how he humbles himself in the history of salvation—but without losing his divinity in the process.[8] The fact that the Son is begotten of the Father in no way implies inferiority or that the Son is subordinate to the Father. When the Son is called "light of light," it is because the Son is "of" the Father, who is "light," but the Father is never "light" without the Son.[9] The two belong eternally together and are therefore equally God. Thus, in Augustine we have a variation on the well-known argument that can be traced back to Origen, which, in short, states that in order to be eternally Father, the Father must also eternally have a Son, who must therefore be begotten with an eternal birth.

7. Augustine, *Answer to Maximinus* 11.

8. Augustine, *On the Trinity* 1.7.14. So-called *partitive exegesis*, as mentioned above.

9. Augustine, *On the Trinity* 6.2.3.

In Cappadocian theology, human relations were often used to illustrate the Trinity. In Augustine, the social analogy is replaced by a more individual, psychological approach, where traces of the whole Trinity are found in each individual human person. There was nothing new in stating that every human being is created in the image of God, but Augustine is creative when it comes to finding traces of the Trinity in the individual human person. For example, when the human mind remembers, understands and loves God, memory, understanding and love are an image of the triune God that humans partake of—not so much because each part reflects each person of the Trinity one to one, but because human relations with the triune God must be characterized by these three.[10] In love there is the one who loves, the one who is loved, and love itself.[11] This is expressed when the New Testament states that "he who abides in love abides in God, and God abides in him" (1 John 4:16). Augustine explains that it is not possible to love someone without also loving love itself, i.e., God.

Augustine also emphasizes that the Father and the Son are each God "in themselves."[12] This may sound like a way of thinking that is at odds with the view that the Father and the Son are what they are only by virtue of their mutual relationship. However, Augustine makes it clear that the Father and the Son are each God. The two are not God only by virtue of their mutual relations. For something to be related, it must also be something in itself. The Father is God in himself, just as the Father is also wisdom and power in himself. The same must be said of the Son. It may seem as if Augustine understands the Father and the Son from an underlying divine being—and this is what has often been criticized.[13] However, the Father not only *has* a divine being, but the Father *is* his divine being. The Father and Son together are one "essence of

10. Augustine, *On the Trinity* 14.12.15.

11. Augustine, *On the Trinity* 8.1.2.

12. Augustine, *On the Trinity* 7.1.1–2.

13. Robert Jenson even argued that Augustine "rejected the Cappadocian doctrine for the sake of his simplicity axiom." Jenson, *Triune Identity*, 119.

essence," says Augustine.[14] This is important because God's being is not, then, something abstract that precedes the divine persons.[15] It is precisely the Father who gives the Son his own being when he begets the Son. As in Cappadocian theology, divine simplicity plays a central role in the argument. The Son derives his divine being from his Father, but because God is one, the two are one being. The Son of God is "God of God" and "light of light," even though the Father and the Son considered separately are each "light."[16] Together they are one light, but only because the Father has passed on his light to the Son, so to speak.

As mentioned above, it is sometimes claimed that Augustinian, "Latin" trinitarian theology is based on the abstract unity of God, while the "Greek" is based on the persons of God. In Cappadocian theology, the Father is the ultimate principle from which the Son and the Spirit have their divinity. The being of God is therefore something personal. Whereas the Eastern emphasis on the communion between the divine persons leads to a more social view of God and humanity, the Augustinian view—it is claimed—leads to the kind of individualism that has come to characterize much of modernity. This may be true to some extent, but it is important not to exaggerate the differences.

While Augustine is famous for finding traces of the trinity in each individual person, the social analogy is not completely absent in Augustine, although it is now applied in the context of the church. Augustine, in arguing against Maximinus, likens the unity of God with that of the church in which "the souls of many humans" have been merged by the Holy Spirit.[17] The charity of the Holy Spirit have made "one heart" of "thousands of hearts," says Augustine, who in this way emphasizes the unity or "catholicity" of the church.

14. Augustine, *On the Trinity* 7.2.3.

15. See Ayres, *Nicea and its Legacy*, 378–79.

16. Augustine, *On the Trinity* 7.3.4.

17. Augustine, *Debate with Maximinus* 12.

Grace Means Free

To Augustine, as in Nicene theology, it is essential for soteriology that the Son of God has the same being as God the Father. This is already clear from Augustine's work on the Trinity. Here he adopts the principle, as mentioned, that we must distinguish between passages that speak of the Son as equal to the Father, on the one hand, and passages that speak of the Son as subordinate to the Father, on the other.[18] The first set of passages refers to the eternal, divine nature of the Son of God, while the latter refers to what the Son of God goes through for us in the history of salvation. When the Father is called greater than the Son in Scripture (John 14:28), it is only because the Son of God has become human for the sake of our salvation—and by doing so mediates between God and humans. This does not, however, make the Son subordinate to the Father in his nature.

Augustine, in his *Handbook on Faith, Hope and Love*, describes how Jesus is "the one mediator" between God and humans, who could only save us because he himself was also God.[19] When the first human, Adam, was created, he needed no intermediary or mediator between him and God. However, sin introduced a chasm between God and humanity. This makes necessary someone who could live and die without sin to reconcile us with God. Jesus could do this because he was divine in his being. Through his birth, life, and death without sin, Jesus has reconciled us to God. However, Augustine adds that there are many aspects of the reconciliation that takes place in Jesus, which he also refers to as the "sacrament of the mediator." The purpose of reconciliation is resurrection to eternal life, but also that humanity's pride can be revealed and thereby healed through what Augustine—perhaps echoing Gregory of Nazianzus—calls the "humility of God."

Augustine draws on the larger theological tradition when he talks about Jesus ransoming humans from death, or conquering death, by going to death himself—an idea that played a role in

18. Augustine, *On the Trinity* 1.7.14.

19. Augustine, *Enchiridion on Faith, Hope and Love* 108.

Origen and Gregory of Nyssa, as outlined above. What stands out from previous theology is Augustine's strong emphasis on human sin understood as pride. This understanding of sin was arguably due to the new fronts that had been drawn up in the dispute with Pelagius on the freedom of the will. Pelagius, according to Augustine, was way too confident in human free will and our ability to choose and do what is right. Sin means that humans are unable to choose and believe God on their own. Sin is pride, and believing that we have the ability to choose God ourselves is just more of the same, namely sin.[20] Augustine has a keen eye for the depth of sin and the necessity of grace. As for the doctrine of the Trinity—which Pelagius did not reject—Augustine's point in his handbook was that by becoming human, God made it clear that only God can reconcile humans through a humility of which sinful humans are not capable.

Perhaps we might even say that Augustine closes a gap in earlier Nicene and Cappadocian theology, which often had a more optimistic view of human free will. If God must become human because humans are unable to save themselves, as held by Nicene theology, we cannot expect humans to be able to choose salvation on their own. We need God's help on all levels. The doctrine of the Trinity implies and supports the understanding that only God can save humans and that salvation is for this reason a gift of grace. As Augustine puts it, no one can be saved without the grace that is not given because of merit, but freely, which is why it is called grace, or *gratia* in Latin.[21]

If faith is a gift of grace, it must be God who decides who should have faith. This is how the doctrine of election and predestination becomes central to Augustine. It is crucial, however, that the Father and the Son are not played off against each other in this—as if Christ wants to save everyone, but unfortunately can only save those whom his Father has predestined for salvation. Trinitarian theology also plays a role here, since the whole Trinity is involved in predestination and election. This is clear in

20. Augustine, *On Grace and Free Will* 38.

21. Augustine, *On Nature and Grace* 4.

Augustine's book *On the Predestination of the Saints.* The works of the triune God are inseparable, there is only one will in God. The Father teaches humans through his Word and Spirit, and all who are in this way taught by the triune God will also believe and come to God.[22] Jesus is predestined as the one in whom the Word of God has united with a human, while the elect are predestined *in* him.[23] Predestination, to this degree, primarily concerns Jesus, who is again the mediator between God and humanity.

It is striking how Augustine deliberately concludes his book on predestination with a christological reflection. The primary example of predestination is the mediator himself, Augustine argues, for it is in him that the Word of God gives human nature a share in the triune God.[24] Christ is truly God, begotten of the Father before all time, but in time he has become human, though without compromising his equality with the Father. It is the same God who has created humans by grace, who now, by grace transforms the evil will of humans into a good one so that they may believe in him. In other words, salvation is a new creation, as Athanasius had also pointed out, and that is why Jesus must be God if he is to save humans.

This is not to say that Augustine invents an entirely new theology. However, it is fair to say that he emphasizes some themes in a new way that lays the foundation for a particular theological tradition. There is an emerging individualism in Augustine, which is also expressed in his introspective approach to faith. The notion of election and predestination plays a role, and the doctrine of a double outcome to salvation and damnation in subsequent theology arguably helped to promote a more individualistic view of the human person. It is no longer so much humanity in general who is created in the image of the triune God, but the individual human, just as salvation no longer concerns humanity collectively, but only the elect.

22. Augustine, *On the Predestination of the Saints* 1.13.

23. Augustine, *On the Predestination of the Saints* 1.31.

24. Augustine, *On the Predestination of the Saints* 2.67. Cf. Hilary, *On the Trinity* 4.37.

Where the Word of God Is, There Is the Trinity

In late medieval nominalism, the doctrine of a double outcome to salvation and damnation became an argument against classical notions of participation. Participatory ontology would give way to theological voluntarism. This would also affect trinitarian theology. William of Ockham (1287–1347) argued that if humans are what they are by participating in a common humanity, then all must be saved or perish collectively. However, since this is not the case—argued Ockham—there can be no collective humanity that individual humans participate in. Whereas the social analogy of Gregory of Nyssa, for example, implied a strong emphasis on the unity of humanity as reflective of the unity of God, the doctrine of a double outcome to salvation and damnation now meant that humans must be seen as separate individuals who are saved or perish individually.

Community between individual persons becomes, to a higher degree, a matter of covenant and will. This makes it difficult to see how we can talk about the divine persons having a common being. Ockham was of the opinion that the doctrine of the Trinity was irrational to natural human logic. The idea of the Trinity as a "paradox," understood as something strange and surprising, was nothing new, but increasingly the Trinity was seen as a contradiction to human reason. The Trinity can, to this degree, not be an object of knowledge, but only of faith. In this respect, it is not surprising if the doctrine of the Trinity gradually loses its significance. Whereas in classical theology it was an attempt to put the gospel into words, it becomes an incomprehensible residue of outdated metaphysical speculation.

It is no wonder, then, that classical trinitarian theology met with new criticism during the Reformation in the 1500s. The radical reformers and the Anabaptists often rejected the doctrine of the Trinity as unbiblical. In many cases, they formulated alternatives similar to views labeled heretical in the early church.[25]

25. For example, many believed that Christ had brought his own "heavenly flesh" with him in the incarnation, while adoptionist views of Christ were also widespread.

Martin Luther and Philip Melanchton were also skeptical about the theoretical formulations of trinitarian theology—but without rejecting the matter at the core of the doctrine of the Trinity. The divinity of Christ was very much a common thread in Lutheran theology: "Where the Word is, there is the Trinity," said Luther in a sermon for Ascension Day using a formulation that sounds like Athanasius.[26] Although Luther can perhaps be said to radicalize the opposition between faith and reason, he did not do away with trinitarian theology for that reason.

That humans are made righteous or justified by grace through faith is a traditional formulation of the main concern of Lutheran theology. Justification is not mentioned in the classical creeds, but this does not mean that Lutheran theology should be seen as an alternative or substitute to Nicene theology. Luther explains in his commentary on Galatians that the core of the doctrine of justification is precisely the article on the divinity of Christ.[27] Only God can triumph over sin and death, but this is why it is necessary, Luther writes, that Christ "in and by himself" is truly and by nature God. Christ is at once a divine and human person who has taken on sin and death for our sake. Therefore, Luther writes, the whole emphasis is on the words "for us."[28]

It is also significant that the Augsburg Confession begins by acknowledging the legacy of the "Nicene Creed." There is one eternal divine being, but three equal divine persons.[29] In Luther's writing on the councils of the fourth century, the divinity of Jesus

26. Luther, *Predigten 1526,* 20:388.24. Although it's the other way round when Athanasius writes that where the Father is, there is also his Word. Athanasius, *On the Council of Nicaea* 11.

27. Luther, *Commentary on Galatians,* 3.

28. Curiously, Luther criticizes "most of the church fathers" for seeing Christ as an isolated individual who was "holy and just for his own sake." It can hardly be, for example, Athanasius, Hilary, or Gregory of Nazianzus that Luther has in mind, as they, like Luther, emphasized what the Son of God has become "for us."

29. Confessio Augustana §1. Here, however, one could argue that this clearly expresses a "Latin" trinitarian theology that speaks first of God's being and then God's persons, rather than a classical "Greek" that speaks "personally" of God as the Father who begets the Son from his own being.

is also crucial.[30] The technical details of the discussions about the Trinity are less important, but Luther affirms the essential point that God became human in Jesus to save humans. Although Luther on several occasions distances himself from traditional concepts of the Trinity as nonsense (literally "sausage talk"), he affirms the heart of the matter. Whether we use the exact words of the Nicene Creed and describe it as the Son of God having the "same being" as the Father is less important. What matters is that the Son is equal to the Father.[31]

What stands out in Luther is an emphasis on faith understood as a relation between the individual believer and God. Our reconciliation with God is a reality through Jesus's death and resurrection for us, but it must be believed in order for us to benefit from it. A good message can only bring comfort and joy if we trust that it is true. Sin and death may have been conquered in Christ, but this reality is nevertheless only effectual for those who believe. The gospel must be true "for me" (*pro me* in Latin), which is arguably also what makes baptism necessary, as baptism is the event in which the gospel is proclaimed *personally* to the baptized.

However, for Luther, the significance of Christ "for us" (*pro nobis* in Latin) was still the precondition for Christ's significance "for me," but in modernity Christianity is gradually individualized to such an extent that the gospel—as in Pietism and Evangelicalism—comes to be primarily about "personal" faith. The individual takes precedence and comes to overshadow the common and collective as the world becomes modern. Theology's preoccupation with the being of God and the Trinity is gradually replaced by faith conceived as a subjective experience of God.

It is hardly surprising that classical trinitarian theology does not play a major role in the modern subjective understanding of faith. When Christianity becomes a matter of a personal relationship of faith, rather than specific doctrines, the old creeds become of less importance. The German philosopher Immanuel Kant, for example, did not believe that the Trinity had any practical

30. Luther, *On the Councils and the Church.*

31. See Helmer, "Between History and Speculation," 151.

significance, and since religion is primarily about morality, trinitarian theology became essentially superfluous or a mere appendix to theology—if it was not simply ignored or rejected altogether as a product of Greek philosophy. However, this seems to leave us with no objective basis for faith. It is not strange, then, if theologians have diagnosed a lack in the modern approach to theology, and instead encouraged a renewed interest in the trinitarian theology of the early church.

AFTERWORD

Jesus of the Comma and the Missing Middle

TODAY, IT HAS BECOME commonplace again to engage with trinitarian theology. In the ecumenical movement in the twentieth century and among Roman Catholic and Orthodox theologians in particular, there has been a desire to reach back to the common basis of faith expressed in creeds such as the Nicene Creed.[1] The Trinity is no longer perceived as a logical absurdity or as remnants of outdated metaphysics, but as a challenge to theology that must rethink tradition in order to speak theologically in the present. A renewed attention to the classical doctrine of the Trinity has also become relevant for discussions that go beyond theology in a narrow sense.[2] The old discussions are still relevant.

In reaction to what was perceived as an overly subjective understanding of faith, trinitarian theology also gained new attention in Protestant theology in the twentieth century—not least in the Neo-Orthodox insistence on the objective side of the gospel, in line with especially Athanasius.[3] This did not, however, mean a return

1. E.g., Rahner, *Trinity.*

2. See, e.g., the recent publication by Milbank et al., *New Trinitarian Ontologies.*

3. E.g., Karl Barth and Thomas F. Torrance.

to traditional "metaphysics." Protestant theologians in particular have emphasized the historical nature of the Trinity, following the theosophical tradition of Jacob Böhme and Hegel, where God is revealed or even becomes himself dialectically through overcoming differences in the world. Traditional philosophical notions of what God is eternally are replaced by a "historicist" theology, where God is what God becomes for us in the history of salvation.[4] Such current attempts to understand the Trinity historically are not, however, without problems. As critics have pointed out, God's identity is made dependent on the evil, sin and death that God overcomes in the history of salvation.[5] It may be better, then, to return to a more "classically" trinitarian theology. God is eternally and immutably the triune God, who as such is love. This is not something that God first becomes in the history of salvation—but salvation consists in the fact that the God who created the world out of love restores broken creation out of that same love.

There are good reasons for engaging with classical trinitarian theology, but doing so requires a consideration of its philosophical assumptions. Recent theological movements, such as Radical Orthodoxy, have emphasized the need to challenge the current (post-) modern worldview with a fundamentally trinitarian thinking. The nominalist rejection of classical ontology has led to increasing individualism, disintegration and even nihilism. We now need to retrieve the notion of participation in the triune God that guided classical Christianity. Trinitarian theology may be said to imply an early "deconstruction" of metaphysics.[6] However, it also offers a positive alternative to post-modernity's preoccupation with differences and contradictions in the world. With its trinitarian notion of unity in diversity, Christian theology has already overcome the metaphysical reduction of everything to one principle, but without making differences the overruling principle instead.[7] Trinitarian ontology implies a "relational ontology" that manages to think

4. See Jenson, *Triune Identity*, 161–85.

5. Hart, *Beauty of the Infinite*, 160–67.

6. Nancy, *Dis-Enclosure*, 35–36.

7. As argued by, e.g, Milbank, "Only Theology Overcomes Metaphysics."

unity and diversity together without doing violence to what is different and distinctive.[8]

Here it should perhaps be noted that trinitarian theology is not so much a matter of "balancing" unity and diversity, since the two are not competing factors on the same plane. Rather diversity is made possible by a unity that is "always already" *in* diversity. The "monarchy" of the Father together with an egalitarian ontology suggests that the unity of being is not an abstract principle that somehow hovers above diversity. That unity is, moreover, presupposed in diversity as a *gift* means that it is not something that we need to "achieve," for example through political or ecumenical work, but rather something that we need to recognize and acknowledge as in a sense already there. The same is true when speaking more specifically about salvation and reconciliation, since—in Nicene theology—these can be seen as in principle already realized in the union of humanity and God in Christ. The kingdom of God is not a matter of ideals that must be realized, but about participating in the *reality* of the Trinity.

This may all be very well "in theory," but it has to be put into practice to be credible, it might be argued. As inhabitants of postmodernity, we can be quite skeptical towards old creeds. Faith is still seen in largely pragmatic terms, as a matter of practice rather than theory. To this degree, it is not irrelevant when theologians have pointed out the absence of ethics in the classic creeds. It is notable, as one author has argued, that the Sermon on the Mount says nothing about what Christians should believe about God, but only something about how they should act and live—and that the Nicene Creed, on the other hand, says nothing about how Christians should live, but a lot about what they should believe.[9] Others have spoken of the "Jesus of the comma," who hides in the commas of the creeds, and the "missing middle," i.e., all that happened between Jesus's birth and death, but which is missing from the

8. Maspero, *Cappadocian Reshaping of Metaphysics.*

9. Meyers, *Saving God from Religion*, 103.

creeds. The creeds should be read in the light of the gospel narratives, rather than the other way around, it is argued.[10]

It may seem reasonable to call for a "moral" component in the classical formulations of faith, seeing that Christianity is, of course, very much about the life we live. However, the theologians of the first centuries were far from indifferent to the practical side of Christianity—as is evident, for example, from the canons of the council in Nicaea (although they can hardly be said to be the object of the church's common "faith" in the same way as the creed). As we've seen, conclusions about the equal worth of all human beings were drawn from Trinitarian theology. Perhaps we could even argue that failing to treat others as equals is, by analogy, a denial of the equality of the divine persons in whose image humanity is created. Trinitarian theology has obvious ethical consequences. The theology of the creeds is not a replacement for the Sermon on the Mount, for example, but the backdrop that gives meaning to it. It is only because Jesus is really God that it makes sense to live as his disciple. The Christian faith is primarily a faith in Christ as the Son of God, not in moral teachings—but this does not mean that Christianity is irrelevant to the life lived. What matters is that the order is right—that we begin with the God who has become human for our salvation.

Nicene theology emphasized that God is the measure of human relations, not the other way around. Theology cannot be based on the believing individual or the community of believers, but must be based on the reality proclaimed by the gospel.[11] In a so-called "post-Constantinian" age, where church and state are no longer closely linked, but where the universal outlook has been replaced by special interests and identity politics, this aspect of classical trinitarian theology has something to offer. The gospel concerns a common reality that applies universally and independently of particular human cultures and identities. However,

10. E.g., Wright, *How God Became King*, 273.

11. As Torrance noted, for Nicene theologians like Hilary, faith was to "stand on the ground of God's own being." Torrance, *Trinitarian Faith*, 19. Hilary, *On the Trinity* 1.18.

it must be actualized and made concrete in particular languages and practices. The task is, then, to think through how trinitarian theology can shape how we perceive the gospel and the church in our specific contexts. The creeds are not just of historical interest, but continue to challenge how we understand the gospel and its implications for church and life.

Bibliography

Alexander of Alexandria. *Letter to Alexander of Thessalonica*. In *The Trinitarian Controversy*, translated and edited by William G. Rusch, 33–44. Sources of Early Christian Thought. Philadelphia: Fortress, 1980.

Arius. *Letter to Alexander of Alexandria*. In *The Trinitarian Controversy*, translated and edited by William G. Rusch, 31–32. Sources of Early Christian Thought. Philadelphia: Fortress, 1980.

———. *Letter to Eusebius of Nicomedia*. In *The Trinitarian Controversy*, translated and edited by William G. Rusch, 29–30. Sources of Early Christian Thought. Philadelphia: Fortress, 1980.

———. *Thalia*. In *Formation of Christian Theology*, translated by John Behr, 2:140–41. New York: St. Vladimir's Seminary Press, 2004.

Athanasius. *De decretis (On the Council of Nicaea)*. In *Nicene and Post-Nicene Fathers of the Christian Church, Second Series*, edited by P. Schaff and H. Wace, 4:149–72. New York: Christian Literature, 1892.

———. *History of the Arians*. In *Nicene and Post-Nicene Fathers of the Christian Church, Second Series*, edited by P. Schaff and H. Wace, 4:270–302. New York: Christian Literature, 1892.

———. *Letter to Adelphius*. In *Nicene and Post-Nicene Fathers of the Christian Church, Second Series*, edited by P. Schaff and H. Wace, 4:575–78. New York: Christian Literature, 1892.

———. *Letters to Serapion on the Holy Spirit*. In *Works on the Spirit: Athanasius and Didymus*, translated by M. DelCogliano et al., 51–137. Popular Patristics Series 43. New York: St Vladimir's Seminary Press, 2011.

———. *On the Councils of Ariminum and Seleucia*. In *Nicene and Post-Nicene Fathers of the Christian Church, Second Series*, edited by P. Schaff and H. Wace, 4:448–80. New York: Christian Literature, 1892.

———. *On the Incarnation*. Translated by John Behr. Popular Patristics Series 44. New York: St. Vladimir's Seminary Press, 2011.

———. *Orations Against the Arians*. In *Nicene and Post-Nicene Fathers of the Christian Church, Second Series*, edited by P. Schaff and H. Wace, 4:306–431. New York: Christian Literature, 1892.

———. *Synodal Letter to the People of Antioch.* In *Nicene and Post-Nicene Fathers of the Christian Church, Second Series*, edited by P. Schaff and H. Wace, 4:483–86. New York: Christian Literature, 1892.

Augustine. *Answer to Maximinus.* In *Arianism and Other Heresies*, translated by Ronald J. Teske, 231–336. Hyde Park, NY: New City, 1995.

———. *Exposition on the Book of Psalms.* In *Nicene and Post-Nicene Fathers of the Christian Church, First Series*, edited by P. Schaff and H. Wace, 8:1–228. Repr. Peabody, MA: Hendrickson, 1995.

———. *Enchiridion: On Faith, Hope, and Love.* Translated by Albert C. Outler. Philadelphia: Westminster, 1955.

———. *On the Trinity.* In *Nicene and Post-Nicene Fathers of the Christian Church. First Series*, edited by P. Schaff and H. Wace, 5:1–228. Repr. Peabody, MA: Hendrickson, 1995.

Aulen, Gustaf. *Christus Victor: An Historical Study of the Three Main Types of the Idea of Atonement.* London: SPCK, 1931.

Ayres, Lewis. *Nicea and Its Legacy: An Approach to Fourth-Century Trinitarian Theology.* Oxford: Oxford University Press, 2004.

Basil of Caesarea. *Against Eunomius.* Edited and translated by Mark DelCogliano and Andrew Radde-Gallwitz. Fathers of the Church 122. Washington, DC: CUA Press, 2014.

Beeley, Christopher A. *Gregory of Nazianzus on the Trinity and the Knowledge of God: In Your Light We Shall See Light.* Oxford: Oxford University Press, 2008.

Behr, John. *The Nicene Faith: The Formation of Christian Theology, Volume 2.* New York: St. Vladimir's Seminary Press, 2004.

———. *The Way to Nicea: The Formation of Christian Theology, Volume 1.* New York: St. Vladimir's Seminary Press, 2001.

Branson, Beau. "One God, the Father: The Neglected Doctrine of the Monarchy of the Father, and Its Implications for the Analytic Debate about the Trinity." *TheoLogica* 6 (2022) 6–58.

Butner, D. Glenn. "Eternal Functional Subordination and the Problem of the Divine Will." *Journal of the Evangelical Theological Society* 58 (2015) 131–49.

Clement of Alexandria. *Christ the Educator.* Edited and translated by Simon P. Wood. Fathers of the Church 23. New York: Fathers of the Church, 1954.

———. *Exhortation to the Greeks. The Rich Man's Salvation. To the Newly Baptized.* Translated by G. W. Butterworth. Loeb Classical Library 92. Cambridge, MA: Harvard, 1919.

Danielou, Jean. *Gospel Message and Hellenistic Culture; A History of Early Christian Doctrine Before the Council of Nicaea, Volume 2.* Westminster: Darton, Longman & Todd, 1973.

Dillon, John. *The Middle Platonists: A Study of Platonism, 80 B.C. to A.D. 220.* London: Duckworth, 1996.

Edwards, Mark. "Is Subordinationism a Heresy?" *TheoLogica* 4 (2020) 69–86.

Ehrman, Bart, ed. and trans. The Apostolic Fathers. 2 vols. Loeb Classical Library 24–25. Cambridge, MA: Harvard University Press, 1912–1913.

Eusebius of Caesarea. *Letter to His Church concerning the Synod at Nicaea*. In *The Trinitarian Controversy*, translated and edited by William G. Rusch, 57–60. Sources of Early Christian Thought. Philadelphia: Fortress, 1980.

———. *The Proof of the Gospel Being the Demonstratio Evangelica of Eusebius of Caesarea*. Translated by William J. Ferrar. New York: Macmillan, 1920.

Glimm, Francis X., et al., trans. The Apostolic Fathers. Fathers of the Church 1. Washington, DC: Catholic University of America Press, 1969.

Gregory of Nazianzus. *The Five Theological Orations*. In *On God and Christ*, translated by F. Williams and L. Wickham, 25–147. Popular Patristics Series 23. New York: St Vladimir's Seminary Press, 2002.

———. *Oration 38*. In *Nicene and Post-Nicene Fathers of the Christian Church, Second Series*, edited by P. Schaff and H. Wace, 7:270–302. New York: Christian Literature, 1892.

Gregory of Nyssa. *Catechetical Discourse*. Translated by Ignatius Green. Popular Patristics Series 60. New York: St Vladimir's Seminary Press, 2019.

———. *Homilies on Ecclesiastes: An English Version with Supporting Studies*. Edited by Stuart G. Hall. Proceedings of the Seventh International Colloquium on Gregory of Nyssa. Berlin: de Gruyter, 1993.

———. *Homilies on the Song of Songs*. Translated by Richard A. Norris. Writings from the Greco Roman World 13. Atlanta: Society of Biblical Literature, 2012.

———. *The Life of Moses*. Translated by A. J. Malherbe and E. Ferguson. New York: Paulist, 1978.

———. *The Lord's Prayer, The Beatitude*. Translated by Hilda C. Graef. Ancient Christian Writers 18. New York: Paulist, 1954.

———. *On Death and Eternal Life*. Translated by Brian E. Daley. Popular Patristics Series 64. New York: St Vladimir's Seminary Press, 2022.

———. *On the Soul and the Resurrection*. Translated by Catharine P. Roth. Popular Patristics Series 12. New York: St. Vladimir's Seminary Press, 1993.

Groh, Dennis C., and Gregg, Robert C. *Early Arianism: A View of Salvation*. Philadelphia: Fortress, 1981.

Hanson, R. P. C. *The Search for the Christian Doctrine of God: The Arian Controversy 318–381*. Edinburgh: T. & T. Clark, 1988.

Harrison, Peter. "I Believe Because It Is Absurd." *Church History* 86 (2017) 339–64.

Hart, David B. *The Beauty of the Infinite: The Aesthetics of Christian Truth*. Grand Rapids: Eerdmanns, 2003.

Hart, David B. "The Myth of Schism." In *Ecumenism Today: The Universal Church in the 21st Century*, edited by Francesca A. Murphy and Christopher Asprey, 95–106. Farnham: Ashgate, 2008.

Helmer, Christine. "Between History and Speculation: Christian Trinitarian Thinking After the Reformation." In *The Cambridge Companion to the Trinity*, edited by Peter C. Phan, 149–69. Cambridge: Cambridge University Press, 2011.

Hilary of Poitiers. *On the Trinity.* In *Nicene and Post-Nicene Fathers of the Christian Church, Second Series*, edited by P. Schaff and H. Wace, 9:40–234. New York: Christian Literature, 1899.

Hippolytus. *Contra Noetum.* Translated by Robert Butterworth. London: Heythrop Monographs, 1977.

Irenaeus. *Against Heresies.* In *Ante-Nicene Fathers: The Writings of the Fathers down to A.D. 325*, edited by Alexander Roberts et al., 1:309–567. Buffalo: Christian Literature, 1885.

———. *On the Apostolic Preaching.* Translated by John Behr. Popular Patristics Series 17. New York: St Vladimir's Seminary Press, 1997.

Jenson, Robert W. *The Triune Identity: God According to the Gospel.* Eugene, OR: Wipf & Stock, 2002.

Justin Martyr. *Dialogue with Trypho.* Translated by Thomas B. Falls, revised and with a new introduction by Thomas P. Halton, and edited by Michael Slusser. Fathers of the Church 3. Washington, DC: Catholic University of America Press, 2003.

———. *The First and Second Apologies.* Edited and translated by Leslie W. Barnard. Ancient Christian Writers 56. New York: Paulist, 1997.

Kahlos, Ritva T. M. "A Misunderstood Emperor? Valens as a Persecuting Ruler in Late Antique Literature." In *Heirs of Roman Persecution: Studies on a Christian and Para-Christian Discourse in Late Antiquity*, edited by Éric Fournier and Wendy Mayer, 61–78. London: Routledge, 2019.

Karamanolis, George. *The Philosophy of Early Christianity.* Abingdon: Routledge, 2021.

Kelly, J. N. D. *Early Christian Creeds.* 3rd ed. London: Longman, 1972.

Kinzig, Wolfram. *A History of Early Christian Creeds.* Berlin: De Gruyter, 2024.

———. *"Zwei neuentdeckte Predigten des Nestorios:* Adversus haereticos de divina trinitate *(CPG 5691) und* In symbolum fidei. *Edition, Übersetzung und Kommentar." Zeitschrift für Antikes Christentum* 24 (2020) 437–89.

Jacobsen, Anders-Christian. *Christ—the Teacher of Salvation. A Study on Origen's Christology and Soteriology.* Adamantiana 6. Münster: Aschendorff, 2015.

Jacobsen, Anders-Christian. "Sophia: The Female Aspect of Christ in Origen of Alexandria." *Open Theology* 10 (2024) 1–7.

Liftin, Bryan M. "Tertullian on the Trinity." *Perichoresis* 17 (2019) 81–98.

Luther, Martin. *Commentary on the Epistle to the Galatians.* Translated by Theodore Graebner. Grand Rapids: Zondervan, 1962.

———. *On the Councils and the Church.* In *Martin Luther's Authority of Councils and Churches.* Translated by Charles B. Smyth. London: William Edward Painter, 1847.

———. *Vorlesungen über Prediger Salomonis und 1. Johannesbrief 1526/27; Predigten 1526.* D. Martin Luthers Werke 20. Weimar: Böhlau, 1883–2009.

Maspero, Giulio. *The Cappadocian Reshaping of Metaphysics: Relational Being.* Cambridge: Cambridge University Press, 2024.

———. *Rethinking the Filioque with the Greek Fathers.* Grand Rapids: Eerdmanns, 2023.

Meyers, Robin R. *Saving God from Religion: A Minister's Search for Faith in a Skeptical Age.* New York: Convergent, 2020.

Milbank, John. "Only Theology Overcomes Metaphysics." *New Blackfriars* 76 (1995) 325–43.

Milbank, John, et al. *New Trinitarian Ontologies, Volume 1.* Eugene, OR: Cascade, 2025.

Munkholt, Maria. "'Light from Light' A Nicene Phrase and Its Use in the Early Church." *The Ecumenical Review* 75 (2023) 249–62.

Myers, Benjamin. "The Patristic Atonement Model." In *Locating Atonement: Explorations in Constructive Dogmatics,* edited by Oliver D. Crisp and Fred Sanders, 71–88. Grand Rapids: Zondervan, 2015.

Nancy, Jean-Luc. *Dis-Enclosure: The Deconstruction of Christianity.* New York: Fordham University Press, 2008.

Origen. *Commentary on the Epistle to the Romans.* Translated by Thomas P. Scheck. Fathers of the Church 103. Washington, DC: The Catholic University of America Press, 2001.

———. *Commentary on the Gospel According to John.* Translated by Ronald E. Heine. Fathers of the Church 88. Washington, DC: The Catholic University of America Press, 1989.

———. *Contra Celsum.* Translated by Henry Chadwick. Cambridge: Cambridge University Press, 1980.

———. *On First Principles.* Translated by John Behr. Oxford: Oxford University Press, 2017.

Osborn, Eric. *Clement of Alexandria.* Cambridge: Cambridge University Press, 2005.

Peterson, Erik. "Monotheism as a Political Problem." In *Theological Tractates,* translated by Michael J. Hollerich, 68–106. Stanford: Stanford University Press, 2011.

Philo of Alexandria. *The Unchangeableness of God; On Husbandry; Noah's Work as a Planter; On Drunkenness; On Sobriety.* Translated by F. H. Colson and G. H. Whitaker. Loeb Classical Library 247. Cambridge, MA: Harvard University Press, 1930.

Plato. *Timaeus. Critias. Cleitophon. Menexenus. Epistles.* Translated by R. G. Bury. Loeb Classical Library 234. Cambridge, MA: Harvard University Press, 1929.

Rahner, Karl. *The Trinity.* New York: Crossroad, 1997.

Ramelli, Ilaria L. E. *The Christian Doctrine of Apokatastasis: A Critical Assessment from the New Testament to Eriugena.* Leiden: Brill, 2013.

———. "Origen's Anti-Subordinationism and its Heritage in the Nicene and Cappadocian Line." *Vigiliae Christianae* 65 (2011) 21–49.

Régnon, Theodore de. *Études de Théologie Positive sur la Sainte Trinité: Première Série—Exposé du Dogme.* Paris: Victor Retaux et Fils, 1892.

Roberts, Alexander, et al., eds. Ante-Nicene Fathers: The Writings of the Fathers down to A.D. 325. 10 vols. Repr. Peabody, MA: Hendrickson, 1994.

Roukema, Riemer. "The Good Samaritan in Ancient Christianity." *Vigiliae Christianae* 58 (2004) 56–74.

Rusch, William G., ed. *The Trinitarian Controversy. Sources of Early Christian Thought.* Philadelphia: Fortress, 1980.

Schaff, P., and H. Wace, eds. Nicene and Post-Nicene Fathers of the Christian Church. 28 vols. in 2 series. Repr. Peabody, MA: Hendrickson, 1995.

Scully, Ellen. *Human Salvation in Early Christianity: Exploring the Theology of Physicalist Soteriology.* Cambridge: Cambridge University Press, 2025.

———. *Physicalist Soteriology in Hilary of Poitiers.* Vigiliae Christianae, Supplements 130. Leiden: Brill, 2015.

Steenbuch, Johannes. *Negative Theology. A Short Introduction.* Eugene, OR: Cascade, 2022.

Tertullian. *On the Flesh of Christ.* In *Tertullian's Treatise on the Incarnation*, translated by Ernest Evans, 4–81. London: SPCK, 1956.

Theophilus of Antioch. *To Autolycus.* Translated by Robert M. Grant. Oxford: Clarendon, 1970.

Torrance, Thomas F. *The Trinitarian Faith: The Evangelical Theology of the Ancient Catholic Church.* London: T. & T. Clark, 1991.

Wright, N. T. *How God Became King: The Forgotten Story of the Gospels.* New York: HarperOne, 2012.

Young, Frances M. *From Nicaea to Chalcedon: A Guide to the Literature and Its Background.* Grand Rapids: Baker Academic, 2004.

Zachhuber, Johannes. *The Rise of Christian Theology and the End of Ancient Metaphysics: Patristic Philosophy from the Cappadocian Fathers to John of Damascus.* Oxford: Oxford University Press, 2020.

Zizioulas, John. *Being as Communion.* New York: St Vladimir's Seminary Press, 1985.

www.ingramcontent.com/pod-product-compliance
Lightning Source LLC
LaVergne TN
LVHW090526110826
845146LV00003B/994

* 9 7 9 8 3 8 5 2 5 5 0 3 0 *